EPHPHATHA

Growing Up Profoundly Deaf and Not Dumb in the Hearing World:
A Basketball Player's Transformational Journey to the Ivy League

————————▼————————

Dr. Thomas M. Caulfield

ISBN: 978-0-9980422-0-6 (pbk.)
      978-0-9980422-1-3 (e-book)
      978-0-9980422-2-0 (audiobook)

Library of Congress Control Number: 2018913587

Photos courtesy of the author unless otherwise noted.

Ephphatha
P.O. Box 2084
Walnut Creek, CA 94595
www.Ephphathabook.com
Printed in the United States of America

DEDICATION

This book is written for all those in the world who are different and find themselves on the outside looking in, wondering how they too can be included.

AUTHOR'S NOTE

At my son's request, I use *Deaf* to acknowledge inclusively the unique challenges and culture of this community of people.

CONTENTS

———▾———

FOREWORD

by Christopher Caulfield

————▼————

When I was in high school I was driven to be the ultimate student athlete. Like many young boys, I wanted to play basketball in college. Given the trajectory I was on in my early teens, I believed this was something I could do. I never saw myself playing in the NBA or even overseas. I knew in my heart that the odds of my playing professionally were astronomical.

It also became very clear to me that if I could, I would like to go to college twice, once to play basketball and the second time to focus most completely on academics. Through an incredible amount of work, I had excelled at both, but it had been a constant struggle. I wanted more time so I could do it all! You see, I had challenges in my life that not many of my peers could ever understand. Challenges that shaped who I was then and who I would become.

Being born Deaf is all I have ever known. Not just Deaf, but profoundly Deaf—I essentially had no hearing at all at birth. Just like playing professional basketball, the odds of me being born with no hearing were in that same realm. It meant many difficult decisions for my parents, challenges in schooling and in my relationships, and hurdles in basketball that others simply never had to face.

You are about to read the true story of a transformational journey that, yes, really did happen to me. My dad kept a secret journal for the first twenty years of my life, knowing that my journey was something remarkable. He hoped someday when he presented it to me that I would enjoy it as his special gift. None of us in our family would have ever imagined that this journal kept for two decades would someday help others learn from our experience and face their own life challenges. The obstacles we faced as a family were at times almost unimaginable, but our strong bond kept us going. Looking back I wonder, if those things hadn't happened to me, would I have achieved all that I have?

As you read *Ephphatha* you might find yourself laughing and crying at the same time. I too still look back with extremely intense emotions. But for me, it is a heartwarming chronicle of overcoming obstacles, making sacrifices, and keeping the faith that this is the path I was meant to take.

Ephphatha is a very powerful word that means to "be opened." Although some people were less than helpful with my progress, the real heroes came into my life via family, medicine, and education. With those special people helping me, my path could "be opened."

So as you read, please remember that for all this to have happened it required people, including me, to "be opened." I might not have set any records being invited to birthday parties when I was growing up. And, yes, both kids and adults were unkind to me. However, my support came from those who did open up. In them, I learned an incredible life lesson. And that is, everyone has the right to be understood. I will remember that forever!

PREFACE

————— ▼ —————

As my wife and I listened to the doctor standing before us, I felt an incredible amount of fortitude for whatever life threw at us. My father had been disabled, and nothing—I mean nothing—stopped him from doing anything he wanted to do. Believe me, his children saw this firsthand with his relentless approach to life. He easily beat me in basketball contests despite his disability, and he was a great writer even though he never had the chance to attend college. Seeing him persevere each and every day gave me a strength that others who had not experienced this adversity didn't know, and now that fortitude was coursing through my body. Yet when the pediatric audiologist informed us that our twelve-month-old son was profoundly Deaf, I wondered if that fortitude would be enough.

Standing there, confused and overwhelmed, I knew one thing for certain: our life was about to get very hard. Almost like a movie, it began to play, and at that early moment in time, just after Christopher's diagnosis, I began to write. I knew what we were about to experience would be challenging and I wanted to capture it all. The journals I kept were the genesis of this book.

The writing came easily at first, but later, in the most difficult times, it also was unbearable. Thankfully, there were the intermittent periods when things were going our way and we actually started having experiences that somewhat resembled those of other families. But it seemed always lurking were serious medical complications that required us to travel coast to coast for treatment.

Besides the medical challenges, we faced a similar wrestling match with the educational system. Whose right was it to choose the intervention strategies that would best help Christopher? It was a struggle that would last more than a decade.

Candidly, I knew we were up against incredible odds when a Catholic nun with more than fifty years of Deaf education to her credit told me, "Dr. Caulfield, in all my years, I am not sure I have seen a family so relentlessly try to combat all the hardships that come with raising a child with such a profound disability." She counseled me to pace myself, adding that if I did choose to scale back my efforts, I could one day look back and honestly say that a great deal had been accomplished. The day she spoke to me, I felt like I was out on a limb cutting with a saw and found myself on the wrong side of the tree branch.

Through it all I continued to write. In one particularly tough period, I remember wanting to post a big, bold warning: If you keep reading this journal, be advised it is not for the faint of heart.

Maybe simply by the grace of God, Christopher turned out to be a phenomenal athlete, and with his talents came all sorts of rights and privileges that he as a Deaf kid never knew existed. Combined with that athletic prowess was Christopher's incredible horsepower academically. With our student athlete by our side, resilience fueled us to combat all of our social, medical, legal, and religious hardships.

As we battled I continued to write, and as we endured for another decade, I knew the important thing to capture was not who was right within our circumstances but rather what was true.

So we persevered, all the while keeping faith that eventually our path would "be opened"—ephphatha—and we could make our way. And maybe when it was all over, our wish would be to have enough resilience remaining in our spirit to bring hope and assistance to others struggling in their own lives.

CHAPTER 1

A Baby Is Born

▼

In late August of 1995, my wife, Jen, and I welcomed our son, Christopher, into the world. Weighing in at almost eleven pounds at birth, he was a huge baby, and I immediately began to plan his future in athletics. The intellectual side of me knew there was no significant correlation between a baby's birth size and his eventual stature, but a dad can dream, can't he?

We had gone to church that Saturday evening, and like most Saturdays, it was family time for us to spend with our four-year-old daughter, Rachel. My wife, who is very tall for a woman, usually moved from room to room in just a few swooping steps. With her standing close to six feet, we joked in our house that she was five-foot-twelve. But with the baby due any day now, she wasn't feeling so energetic as she played with Rachel. When she found me in the family room and casually stated, "Tom, my water broke," the scene abruptly changed. Instead of hanging around the house, we dropped Rachel at a friend's place and headed to the hospital.

While the contractions were still far apart, I had time to take in my surroundings. I was amazed to see how much the labor and delivery room looked like a hotel suite. I mean, it had a TV, a very comfortable recliner, and a great view! Heck, it was kind of like Club Med, as they even asked if I needed anything to eat or drink.

The mood changed once again when those contractions became stronger. I shifted into my stand-by-the-bedside position, ready for those powerful grips I remembered my wife putting on my hand with the birth of our daughter. As things became even more intense, my wife's Club Med bed suddenly converted into operating room equipment. Various carts were unveiled and brought closer to her bedside with all the monitors, tubes, and attachments ready to roll. We were not in Club Med anymore!

As my wife's pain began to rise, a casual request was put in for an epidural. In the nicest way possible, the nurse said, "You are not quite dilated enough yet." Within the hour my wife more assertively requested the epidural. Request denied. At that point I witnessed for the second time something come over my wife. Ever the diplomat at work and in her ways at home, she now had the look in her eyes of being possessed. So there we were, a mild-mannered Mrs. Caulfield suddenly looking like she could hurt someone if they didn't give her that epidural.

Soon after that, a collision of words was inevitable. It went like this: Nurse asks nicely, "So how are you doing?" Possessed woman responds with a voice I had never heard before, "Give me that damn epidural." I thought, "Oh boy, I hope they don't kick us out of here." Luckily the doctor arrived at that time and approved the pain management request.

Once the drugs were working, things moved to serious labor and for the next four hours it was relentless physical exertion on my wife's part. Our son came into the world looking good!

Although the doctors must have performed a whole battery of tests during Christopher's stay in the hospital, our family saw his ten perfect fingers and toes and happily went home. After all, we had done this same drill four years ago with the birth of our daughter. Now she was a big sister!

Christopher at three months

When Christopher arrived home from the hospital, Jen and I were consumed with the responsibility of having two children. We were both working parents who knew in our hearts that we had to give our family the utmost priority during this busy time in our lives. I had witnessed significant levels of dysfunction in my immediate family due to overzealous, job-oriented adults who pushed the career path accelerator without first checking the rearview mirror to see where their kids were. We refused to repeat that mistake.

Many respected child development specialists had extensively commented on the topic. In the early 1990s, we attended an event at our local college's basketball arena to hear a nationally known child psychiatrist speak. Our daughter was to be born later that year and we were eager for information. After the speech, a woman in the audience stood up and asked a huge question: "What is the best way to raise children?"

I thought, "Man, how could anyone answer that?" I mean the complexity of that question could easily have rivaled, What is the meaning of life? I sat in the audience with all sorts of existential anxiety settling into my body. But to my surprise, the good doctor responded as easily as could be. The key to raising children, he said, was to have both parents involved in the process. He added that it would be best for the children's early developmental years if both parents were able to work half-time. In this day and age, that kind of an arrangement could be tough financially for a lot of people. While the doctor acknowledged that financial strain can have an impact on families, he still believed their children would be better off developmentally in the long run. Well, after I heard that, it was as if I had discovered the Holy Grail of parenting. I had grown up in a poor, Irish Catholic family in Chicago, and we had really known how to stretch a buck. I was not afraid of financial strain. I believed the doctor's advice would work for my own family and wanted to give it a try.

Later that night, however, I pondered how I could put the speaker's advice into practice. Could we really put our careers in neutral? I said to myself, "Wait, I have dreams too!" I had just graduated with a doctorate in my field, and I was ready to make my move on the world. But I couldn't ask my wife to stay home full-time. She had just earned a professional degree herself. There was no way she would want to put on the brakes so soon.

Sitting in the living room, we talked over how we wanted to raise our children together. We both had aspirations, but we also saw the value in the doctor's advice. We came to the conclusion that it would be best if each of us could work part-time. I was able to do this because a new business opportunity had recently come my way. Thankfully, my wife's workplace was also supportive of her working a twenty-hour week. It was a done deal. The two of us were off on our co-parenting quest for the perfect life.

————▼————

Before having children, Jen and I took in and nurtured a couple of cats. After that successful experience, the two of us believed we were ready for an even larger challenge. Our daughter, Rachel, was born in 1991, and my wife and I had the time of our lives during her early formative years. Learning had come easily for Rachel, and she had been eager for the start of preschool. Unbeknownst to us, our little redheaded daughter would be instrumental in helping us raise Christopher.

Rachel at four years old with Christopher

At the age of four, Rachel had performed exceptionally on a battery of educational placement tests, demonstrating she was more than up to the challenge of a highly selective laboratory preschool in our college town. She was a natural, too, in the support role for her mother. Those stories of the jealous older sibling went out the window at our home. Rachel, ever the altruist, made me feel just plain lucky to be part of such a loving and giving family!

Christopher's temperament as an infant was different from Rachel's right from the start. Whereas Rachel had been a laid-back baby, Christopher was extremely active and explored everything that came anywhere near his grasp. Rachel was the perfect helper and did whatever it took to make sure Christopher was comfortable during his first year of life. Our family had a great deal going on, and we have all the family videos to prove it. However, the direction of our lives would soon be changing.

Shortly before Christopher's first birthday, I received a call at work from my wife. Jen never calls me at work, so I had a feeling something was up. I answered the phone and after our usual greetings she very calmly said, "Christopher hasn't been turning his head to noises around the house."

I was confused at first. "Say that again?"

"I'm sure it's nothing. He just isn't really responding to sounds in the house. Or out of the house, either."

You can be sure I was not as calm as she was. I left my desk and headed home immediately.

When I reached home, Jen and I strategized how to test our son's hearing. I wish I could say we performed sophisticated hearing analyses to determine what might be happening, but in reality, we banged pots outside of Christopher's crib while he slept. The activity seemed heartless, but we feared the worst and needed to relieve our anxiety. Throughout all the noise, Christopher remained asleep that night. My wife and I were stunned. Surely, this couldn't be happening. The next morning we called our local medical clinic for help. Neither Jen nor I spoke the D word in the days leading up to Christopher's medical appointment.

Three days later, with Rachel in preschool, Jen and I drove with our small son to the doctor's office. Our pediatric neurologist prided himself on bonding with his toddler patients with not only a pleasant disposition but also a very colorful lab coat with Disney characters embroidered on it. "We're in good hands here," Jen assured me with a nod. We both tried to relax, for Christopher's sake. We didn't want him to pick up on our anxiety and get scared. When the doctor entered the room, Christopher's eyes locked in on that fun lab coat and all the other vibrant pictures the good doctor had posted in the room and he was all smiles. We were off to a good start!

The doctor said his hellos, then pulled a tuning fork out of his lab coat. Christopher gave it a quick glance before returning to his visual scan for more interesting stimuli nearby. The doctor flicked the tuning fork and it began to hum. He then brought the tuning fork around the sides of Christopher's head in quest of a reaction. I too hoped for a response, but Christopher took no notice.

With that, we were off to an otologist for a full-blown hearing test. No one had used the D word yet, and I wondered if this visit would be the day. The medical model and all of its exhaustive techniques seemed to be narrowing in on something. At the same time, I was gradually getting to the point where I just wanted to scream "DEAF" in an attempt to own it.

In one bit of luck, the medical clinic in our town was quite large and thus one can easily span numerous divisions of medicine in less than a five-minute walk. Upon arrival at the otologist's office, we first met with an audiologist who asked us a series of questions. At the end she asked, "Are any of you claustrophobic?" She then explained that we would be in a small soundproof booth. "Some people get anxious in there," she said.

Jen and I looked at each other. "We'll be fine," Jen said, but we had no idea how Christopher would feel in there.

As we walked into the booth, I was reminded of a recording studio that you might try to fit in your closet. High-tech gadgets surrounded us. Jen and I each took a chair, and Christopher sat on my lap while we waited for the test to begin. We had been told a series of sounds or tones would be pumped into the booth in an attempt to elicit a response from Christopher. We could see the audiologist through the glass sitting in front of an electronic panel with her special headphones on. Once again Jen and I tried to contain our nervousness.

"Okay, Mr. and Mrs. Caulfield, we're going to start the test now," the audiologist said through the sound system. And then the tones came in. Each one lasted just a moment before the next one sounded. Over and over for what seemed like an hour the tones came and went, with the audiologist meticulously taking notes every step of the way. I watched the audiologist for some sort of facial expression that would indicate a favorable result, but she remained stoic and professional the whole way through. As I stared through the glass I couldn't help but display a bland affect back. We left that afternoon still unsure of what the test had revealed.

A few days later we were asked to return to the clinic to learn more about the test results. We were shown into an exam room and began our wait. After some time, the doctor walked into the room and without hesitation said, "Your son is profoundly DEAF."

Although I had been anticipating this diagnosis, my mind was not ready. As my brain took in the big D word, my mouth rapidly fired out numerous questions. I had been bottling up my fears and now they came tumbling out. At last I asked the audiologist, "Will Christopher ever be able to receive any sort of an education?"

That's when I noticed there was a team of at least four professionals in the room with us, including an audiologist. This group was ready to support us in our time of need. I vaguely recall the answer to my education question involving the word *main-streaming*. I had graduated from grade twenty, and I honestly had never heard the term. It probably wouldn't have mattered anyway because, even though it had only been a short time since I had been told of Christopher's diagnosis, I was pretty sure I

Christopher and Jennifer

Rachel, Tom, and Christopher

was heading into shock. I asked myself, "What type of life will Christopher have? Will he ever get married? How will he learn to talk if he can't hear?"

At that moment I thought I needed to display undeniable fortitude, which wouldn't allow me to feel any sadness about Christopher's deafness. If Christopher ever asked me if I had felt sad when he had first been diagnosed, I wanted to be able to respond with an honest, "No." Would that answer be truthful? I sure hoped it would be. I guess I wanted more than ever for our family to lead our lives in such a way that I would be able to respond to Christopher in this manner if needed. I would never want him to believe that I had wished for him to be any other way. As I sat feeling stunned in that doctor's office, I was sure of one thing: life was about to get much more challenging for our family.

———▼———

After we received Christopher's diagnosis, we talked to the doctor about our options. Hearing aids were the first stop. Christopher was always a happy kid who loved to see and do new things. Being fitted for hearing aids was not one of them. To make a hearing aid that fit comfortably, a technician first had to make a mold of Christopher's ear. Making the mold required goopy stuff to be inserted into each ear and held in place until it set. Ear one went smoothly, but when it came time to do ear two, Christopher wiggled and fought us. Ultimately he had to be restrained. Who could blame him? No one would want someone to stick rubbery stuff in their ear.

At our next visit, we received the hearing aids along with proper instruction on how to insert them. We left, feeling nervous and hopeful, ready to see how good those puppies were. Christopher spent most of the day taking them out and investigating them before placing them in his mouth.

Christopher very much disliked wearing the hearing aids, and getting them fitted in his ears each morning was a physical and emotional struggle. After several days, Jen couldn't take it anymore, and I quickly absorbed it as my morning duty.

Going out in public presented us with more new challenges. I was continually amazed at how many people stared at Christopher. Clearly they had never seen hearing aids on such a small child. Generally they appeared to feel sad for Christopher, but he didn't mind at all. He simply returned each of their gazes with a smile. I wondered at what age he would begin to take those extended gazes personally.

Over the next weeks and months the hearing aids continued to be a problem and soon I began to feel sorry for the hearing-impaired adults who had to wear them, because, in my opinion, those dang hearing aids were the worst. We needed to find a different solution.

CHAPTER 2

A New Beginning

▼

Our first miracle happened when Christopher was about thirteen months old. Jen and I learned that a new school was opening adjacent to our local hospital. It was called the St. Joseph Institute for the Deaf. I thought, "What the heck! The Catholics are going to save us from our misery at last." In a way I felt I in particular deserved it. I had been a good boy growing up and had survived parochial school.

Photo Courtesy of the St. Joseph Institute for the Deaf

St. Joseph was loaded with history. In the 1800s, French nuns founded a school for the Deaf in St. Louis and began educating the youth. Society was not nearly as compassionate toward people with disabilities hundreds of years ago as compared to today, so I thanked God for the Holy Order of Sisters of St. Joseph de Carondelet. They had cared enough to make a difference in the world. I still remember the birthday card they sent to me shortly after we first met them. It simply said, "Dear Thomas, The world is blessed for having you as part of it." Who wouldn't want to get to know the people who had sent such an uplifting message?

The school's mission was to join with our local hospital, which already had a significant reputation in the Midwest for working with Deaf children. Their vision was to provide a preschool option for Deaf children where they could be together in a learning environment with hearing kids. Like many Catholic-based educational systems, they had structure built in to the max. Break-out instructional sessions and speech therapy for the Deaf children would be scheduled separate from their hearing peers. And there was no shying away from the goal of St. Joseph's: front-load intensive speech therapy in ongoing one-on-one sessions to give the children their best shot at learning to speak. At the same time it was also essential to provide daily access to hearing students who would model age-appropriate levels of speech and listening comprehension. Christopher was the first student enrolled in our local St. Joseph School for the Deaf, and Lord willing, I hoped he would turn out to be the school's best student.

While we were grateful for the opportunity to send Christopher to a school so attuned to his needs, it came with a hefty price tag. To be sure, that first school bill for

Christopher's tuition and therapy services was comparable to an Ivy League education, and our insurance would pay for only a portion of it. I sincerely didn't know how we would pay for it. But I thought, "Don't look back. Just get the money to cover the critical therapy." I sounded *like* I was planning to rob a bank!

The staff at St. Joseph's was great and we did everything we could to make it work, but after Christopher's third month there, the clinic staff called us in for a conference. "I'm sorry to tell you Christopher has been making very little progress with his hearing aids," the school director said. We learned he had so little residual hearing—the ability to sense any sound—that even the best hearing aids in the world would have been ineffectual for him. My wife and I were devastated, and I began to lose all hope for Christopher to learn to speak or hear even just a little. The school medical personnel, however, proposed a solution.

"Are you familiar with cochlear implants?" they asked. They then explained all about this revolutionary device that had helped hundreds of Deaf people to hear for the first time. They made no promises but said it might help Christopher with his hearing.

Jen and I were intrigued by the cochlear implant idea, but the school described the operation to install the device as "more than intense." Our son was just sixteen months old and the idea of him having surgery made us very nervous. We went home that day with a lot to think about.

Truth be told, after learning that the dang hearing aids were no good to us, we literally in a day moved into complete research mode on these bionic devices called cochlear implants. We scheduled an appointment with a doctor and counted the days until we could learn more about the implant process.

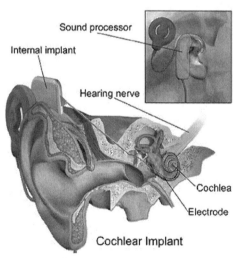

Cochlear Implant

Blausen.com staff (2014) "Medical Gallery of Blausen Medical 2014" Wiki Journal of Medicine 1 (2). DOI: 10.15347/wjm/2014.010 ISSN 2002-4436

At our appointment, the doctor explained that the surgery would be a two- to three-hour outpatient procedure. The surgeon would take an electrode array and implant it through Christopher's cranium down to his cochlea. I was naïve and first had to be told what a cochlea was! A cochlea, the doctor explained, is a part of the inner ear that is about the size of an aspirin tablet. It is fully developed at birth, and its internal network is quite complex. In a hearing child, the cochlea takes vibrating pulses from the eardrum and transmits them to the hair cells within the fluid of the organ itself. Then, the auditory nerve, which is attached to the end of the cochlea, transmits the electrical pulses to the brain. Christopher's deafness was congenital, so the electrode array would bypass his cochlea and transmit the impulses directly to his auditory nerve. My wife and I also learned that a magnetic microphone would be attached to the exterior of Christopher's skull. The microphone would send sound to his implant for decoding, and the sound would then go directly to his brain via his auditory nerve. He would have to wear an external speech processor as well. The processor worked with the transmitter, relaying sound messages from the microphone to the brain. We definitely thought the procedure sounded bionic, as if it had come from the pages of a science-fiction book.

The clinic staff gave us plenty of time to consider the medical procedure. If Jen and I decided to go ahead with the operation, Christopher's surgery would be part of a national experimental trial that only included children under the age of twenty-four months. In Christopher's case, the doctors wanted him to be eighteen months old at the time of his surgery.

Before we made our final decision, I was off to the medical science library at our local university to learn more about what this sci-fi bionic implant was all about. I discovered that surgeons in both the United States and England had been implanting these devices for almost two decades, but my research also showed that Jen and I would be rolling the dice on this particular experimental trial. The literature discussed a few of the surgery's complications. The most serious one was the small risk of a surgeon damaging the patient's facial nerve, which would cause facial paralysis.

When Jen and I met other parents of profoundly Deaf children, they asked, "When did you first find out your child was Deaf?" and "When will you have the implant

Christopher at first birthday

procedure done?" These parents believed that implant surgery was best done when a child was very young. This was also data driven, as the research indicated significant differences between children who received implants around two years of age versus those who received them between five and seven years of age. The message: Christopher needed this surgery *now*.

The next few weeks sped by, and my wife and I finalized our decision to go ahead with Christopher's surgery. We had a mere six weeks until Christopher would turn eighteen months old and get his cochlear implant. Shortly before his surgery date, Christopher caught a cold and his surgery had to be postponed a week. Jen and I were anxious, but we knew we couldn't turn back now! After all, I had practically lived at the medical science library for the past weeks on end reading every piece of literature on cochlear implants I could find. We were committed to trying it for our son.

The day of surgery arrived, and I thought we were really due for some good things to happen to us. We had this great school set and ready to roll and now we just needed

Christopher to be given the ability to hear through this implant. We tried to be emotionally prepared for a positive outcome. Christopher was not nearly as apprehensive as Jen and I were. Unlike his parents, he had no idea what was at stake.

The surgery team representative checked in with us after the first hour of Christopher's scheduled procedure. She told us that things were going well, and the surgeon would be setting the device at the implant site soon. She also explained that the surgeon in this case had to do a great deal of drilling through Christopher's skull to create the pathway for the tiny electrode array to innervate his aspirin-sized cochlea. We thanked her for being so open with what was happening to our little boy.

After that initial update, however, we heard nothing more from the surgery team. The three-hour window for the procedure came and went. After waiting another hour, my wife and I began to fret. Finally, the surgeon, looking visibly shaken himself, met with us. I fought through my worst fears as the surgeon, in a slow, almost methodical tone, asked us to step into a small conference room to talk. I knew something was dreadfully wrong. *Please, God, let Christopher be alive.*

The surgeon hesitated in a clear attempt to gather his composure before speaking to us. My heart immediately went out to the man. I could sense that an operation he had performed hundreds of times before had not gone as expected. Now I wanted to know what had him so upset.

"The implant was successfully placed into Christopher's cochlea," he began. I held my breath for what was coming next. "During the surgery, the facial nerve on the left side of your son's face was nicked. That side of his face is not moving."

My head was trying hard to process this and questions came fast. We had known this was a risk, but how did it happen? According to the doctor, there was no way to prevent it. Christopher's facial nerve was simply not in the correct anatomical place.

I saw that the doctor was becoming more anxious. I perceived him thinking he had disabled our son all over again. I resolved not to ask him any further questions at that time. I wanted to get to Christopher, who was just coming out of anesthesia. The surgeon's final words to my wife and me were that he would send a nurse to be with us and Christopher. The nurse would give us some medical tape to place over Christopher's left eye. "The facial nerve that was nicked also controls eye function," he explained, answering our unasked question. That meant Christopher's eyelid might need to be taped, since it may not be moving normally.

My wife and I entered the curtained-off area where Christopher was resting. His head was wrapped with a huge white bandage resembling a turban. He attempted to smile up at us with one eye partially closed. His smile on the left side of his face drooped, as did our hearts. A million thoughts raced through my mind at that moment. It was as if I was reliving the day when we had been told he was Deaf. All I could muster was a silent scream inside my head. Christopher was a special child, I surmised, given all of this hardship he was being forced to endure. While I wasn't the type of person who usually whined about things, I began to wonder just how much more Jen and I could take. About two hours later, we left the hospital with Christopher, bundles of tape, and new worries about where we were headed.

As the weeks progressed, my wife and I became consumed with two hopes. One was for Christopher to hear, and the other was for his beautiful face to somehow regain its original symmetry. We also couldn't help but feel sad for Christopher's doctor. We knew that he had already helped hundreds of kids regain their hearing, which had changed those kids' lives in a positive way forever. In our case, we would just have to wait and see what the future held for Christopher.

A few weeks after the surgery, it was time to have Christopher's sutures removed. Jen and I had hoped and prayed for Christopher's paralysis to improve, but sadly, there was yet to be any change other than the eyelid, which he seemed to be able to control just a little more.

Rather than fret over what we couldn't change, we directed our attention to a new issue. The doctor informed us that he would soon turn on the electrode array that had been implanted in the left side of Christopher's cranium. This would be done by connecting a dime-sized magnetic device to the exterior of Christopher's skull. A small microphone within the magnetic device would, hopefully, pick up environmental sounds as well as speech. If all worked well, the speech would be transmitted down a wire within a millisecond to the speech processor that Christopher wore on his belt. Then, the sound would be converted to an auditory impulse that would relay the message to Christopher's brain. It was that last "to the brain" part that really caused Jen and me the most concern. In order for Christopher to hear sound, the internal transfer of auditory impulses would have to work within his brain. Thankfully, his doctors already knew the external portion of Christopher's implant was working due to lab testing. The unknown was the electrode array that went down Christopher's cochlea and its connection to the distal end of his auditory nerve. Jen and I had seen films of other children reacting to their implants being turned on. Some children cried, some giggled, and others did nothing. I was not at all surprised by the "do nothing" group, since those toddlers had been Deaf since birth and didn't know what to make of sound. I hoped in my heart that Christopher would at least show some reaction when his implant was turned on. Our family definitely needed something positive at this point in our journey.

As we traveled to our appointment that day, I went back in time to those claustrophobic auditory booths where Christopher was first diagnosed. Those were difficult times and we had hoped to put them behind us. Yet, half a year later and again the question of the day was, would Christopher respond to sound? We didn't know how they planned to test his hearing this time. Would we be back in that booth again? We hoped not, given those memories.

We walked into the office—Jen, Christopher, and I—and the mystery was resolved. The external portion of the implant was sitting on the table in an open office area, waiting to be programmed with an adjacent computer. After a few short tests, the implant was gently placed over Christopher's left ear and its magnet adhered to the exact placement of the internal device. The moment had finally come. We took the lead from the implant team and when all of Christopher's equipment was turned on, his response to various sounds was . . . nothing. My wife and I were left clinging to the thought that we had at least been told of the possibility that Christopher might react in this manner. Searching further for a positive note, we realized that many Deaf children initially had these same results and later spoke just fine. At the end of the appointment, the best we could muster was a, "Gee, I hope this works."

Over the coming months, we did notice Christopher showing a certain level of awareness. His eyes would open wider when a sound was introduced into his environment. But we still didn't know how effective the implant would turn out to be.

———▼———

After the cochlear implant was turned on, we returned Christopher to school for speech therapy. From the start, Jen and I chose to be highly involved in the process. We were amazed at the dedication of the speech pathologists who worked in the school. The therapists began by introducing Christopher to very small amounts of sound at a time. His first task was to learn the "baa" sound. Sitting across from Christopher, the therapist would wind up a toy sheep and repeat "baaa" over and over. "Baaa, baaa." Christopher did not seem impressed. I on the other hand was continually astounded by the therapists' determination. Despite little sign of improvement, they kept right at it. Christopher took almost a month to learn the "baaa" sound. At that glacial pace, I wondered if there would be enough time in Christopher's early childhood for him to learn all of the essential sounds and be successful in the school.

That level of intensive speech therapy went on for six months. At last, Christopher started to respond. We were stunned. Our son was learning to speak! Like Pavlov's dogs, Jen and I were reinforced and had a desire to work even harder for Christopher. Our mission was now very clear. It would take the two of us, the team of speech therapists (or speech terrorists, as we called them, since they were so relentless), Christopher's ability, and a great deal of faith in God to get us through this endeavor.

———▼———

As Christopher aged, I could see another battle looming on the horizon. The support services center in our city had given our family commendable help up until Christopher turned three. After that birthday, however, things changed. We had discovered the methodology called oral education, which completely relied on teaching children how to speak and listen with little, if any, use of sign language. With his implant, Christopher could now hear sounds at twenty-five to thirty decibels. (Without the implant, his decibel level skyrocketed to one hundred and ten, similar to the noise from a jet engine.) Since most people hear at about twenty decibels, we were confident he could handle the challenge of communicating without sign language. But the city's support services did not believe in this teaching method. They stood on their methodology working exclusively with sign language, and we were firm on oral education. It soon became clear that my wife and I were philosophically opposed to this latest support service group's teaching methodology. We turned for support to the Alexander Graham Bell Association, an internationally known nonprofit group that emphasizes helping Deaf children to thrive in mainstream society. We also sought the help of attorneys committed to fighting for children with disabilities. When the dust settled, we were extremely happy: we would be able to teach our son in the way we felt was best. Christopher is who he is today because of that outcome.

From that moment on, the agenda was intensive speech and language therapy with no looking back. Christopher was bombarded with constant speech therapy both at home and at school. My wife and I also enrolled Christopher in day care center classes so he could be continuously surrounded by hearing kids who modeled excellent language skills. Our medical clinic's intervention team regularly tested Christopher as well. It soon became obvious that three-year-old Christopher was almost one and a half years behind in his speech. In other words, he had the speech ability of a one-and-a-half-year-old. I wish I could say that his listening comprehension was the same, but having gone in and out of the day care center, I knew his listening skills were probably closer to that of a one-year-old. Without the listening skills, Christopher would be delayed in schooling as well. Jen and I did not want to wait until he was seven years old before we sent him to kindergarten. I didn't know how we would do it, but our incredible goal was to get Christopher completely ready for kindergarten within the next two years.

The good news was that Christopher's single words had begun the transition to three-word utterances. This meant that his implant was definitely doing its job. Better yet, Christopher's immersion with hearing peers had turned out to be successful. Jen and I also had experimented by enrolling Christopher in a preschool program at our local community college. He was doing so well in the program that he was able to continue spending four hours a day with the hearing kids there. We had always thought that if Christopher could perform well in small groups of hearing peers in a fairly quiet environment, he would be able to pick up on a fair amount of verbal information. This idea had been working out so well for Christopher that my wife and I were "dancing on the tables" once we saw his results.

With just nine months left before the start of kindergarten, our strategy was for Christopher to continue at the community college preschool in the mornings and then attend a university lab preschool with hearing peers in the afternoons. Our daughter, Rachel, had also attended the university lab school and we were highly impressed with its teaching methods, diversity, and the fantastic student-to-teacher ratios. Given the laboratory environment, there were plenty of graduate students from the university continuously involved in the classrooms, which made it an educationally vibrant atmosphere. We also managed to squeeze in speech therapy for him each day. I sometimes wondered if we were pushing Christopher too hard, but the reality was that his brain was responding well. He continuously showed us he was completely up for the challenges.

The year was progressing quickly, and Christopher's achievements in speech and hearing comprehension were astounding. Unfortunately, his facial paralysis had not improved. At that time Jen and I viewed the slight dip on the left side of his face as just a rough break in life. Although in other circumstances it may have been a high priority, in our family it was secondary. Talk about engaging in triage in our own family.

I wondered at times if we would have agreed to let Christopher undergo the cochlear implant surgery had we known that it would lead to his facial paralysis. Now that he was four, we noticed Christopher was becoming self-conscious about how his face looked. He intentionally began presenting only one side of his face to the cameras during photos. We realized it was time to seek medical help.

Our first move was to see if we could find a specialist who worked exclusively with facial nerve damage. We discovered a doctor at Stanford University who had been involved with some facial nerve restorative work. We decided to take the kids to visit some relatives in California and then swing by Stanford. Our main goal was to see what another professional group thought about Christopher's facial paralysis.

Upon our arrival at Stanford, we learned the best and brightest were in fact located in good old Palo Alto. The doctor's office was very small, and I had to stand during the appointment. The doctor, however, quickly got down to business. "Christopher does seem to have the ability to open and close his eye," he told us as Christopher sat in front of him. "If you look closely, you'll see his left cheek does elevate a fraction while his left upper lip is motionless." Our hearts lifted some to hear that news, but it was short-lived. Given what he had seen, the doctor concluded that his office would not consider performing any facial surgery on Christopher after all.

On the one hand, I was relieved the doctor thought Christopher was doing fairly well, but on the other hand, I thought saying no facial improvement could be gained via surgery was too definitive. I wanted further information and spent my winter break researching. That's when I discovered another facial nerve center, this one at the University of Pittsburgh.

We made three visits to the University of Pittsburgh and each was practical and gratifying. The doctors videotaped Christopher's face and hooked him up to a device that measured the biofeedback of his involved facial muscles. We were also able to meet with a physical therapist. Overall, the testing indicated that Christopher's paralysis was not complete. In fact, he had as high as 20 percent muscle capability in select facial muscles. His cheek muscle demonstrated the least paralysis, and his tiny upper lip muscles had the most. It was fascinating watching the specialist graph the left side of Christopher's facial muscles and then compare those to the muscles on his right side. The differences between the two were dramatic, and the doctor suggested physical therapy might enhance Christopher's muscle movement.

The University of Pittsburgh Medical Department also believed Christopher's facial movement was not high enough to warrant performing surgery. My wife and I were grateful for the doctor's assertion that Christopher's condition was "not that bad," but we were also extremely concerned with the fact that Christopher had become so self-conscious about his asymmetrical face. Regardless of our worries, our family left the University of Pittsburgh that day with plenty of exercises that we agreed to faithfully practice with Christopher.

How many other families have dealt with a personal health crisis similar to that of our son? Like anything else, I suppose it varies and is somewhat the luck of the draw. As I lived through my own struggles, I had noticed there seemed to be a continuum. The more I got to know individual families, the more I understood all that they, too, had experienced.

Perhaps this lesson came home to our family the most when we volunteered at the Swann Special Care Center in our town. Every Saturday morning we visited with severely disabled kids who would spend their entire lives in the residential facility. The Swann team did a fantastic job of working with its residents. The patients' afflictions were as severe as one could imagine. Their chronological ages were anywhere from five to forty years old, but most of them developmentally functioned as toddlers.

Our family was deeply saddened the first time we visited the residents but then we met little Timmy. Always smiling and in such a carefree state just wanting to sit in his wheelchair and be a part of the group activities, Timmy had beautiful blue eyes that darted up, down, and all around the room while his head did not move. Just saying his name caused him to open his hand—his signal to welcome you to shake with him. There was no dialogue between us when we met on Saturday mornings, just my hand coming in contact with his and feeling that grasp of his young hand on mine. Our encounter was always brief and he was always the first to release his grip. How peaceful that was for me, since I for sure wouldn't be the one to let go first.

Volunteering at Swann, we had a hard time emotionally reconciling the state of these young people. It was an ominous thought that these kids were brought to this facility and would essentially live there and some would die there as well at a very young age. We never did get over it when from one week to the next, one young person might no longer be at the center. As our visits continued, however, we found that the residents greatly enjoyed our presence, and the staff really valued our family's volunteer efforts as well.

I had underestimated just how much this one volunteer experience could do to help our family put Christopher's disability into perspective. Truthfully, it had become easy for us all to feel sorry for ourselves. After we saw the severity of the children's disabilities at the Swann Center, our family could honestly say, "We will take Deaf."

CHAPTER 3

MAINSTREAM

---▼---

Christopher's immersion with hearing peers at the preschool came to an end later that year. To cap off the academic year, the St. Joseph School for the Deaf held a large graduation party. It was difficult to believe that Christopher had been enrolled at the school for nearly four years. Kindergarten would be here before we knew it.

The following weekend, our family held our own graduation party for Christopher. Reporters from two local TV stations attended the party. After hearing about Christopher, they had contacted us to learn more about his amazing story and asked if they could interview us at the party. It became very clear upon their arrival they wanted to see and show their viewers how this Deaf kid had gotten so far along and was about to enter kindergarten with his peers. Our family liked to maintain our privacy; thus, it was tough allowing the reporters to conduct their interviews. Nonetheless, we had endured many physical and emotional hardships, and we wanted to share our experiences in order to give back to the community. Our hope was to help and give hope and support to other families who had either directly experienced deafness themselves or who knew of others in a similar situation.

Despite our concerns, the television interviews were a great success. The interviews led Christopher and me to speak at various educational institutions and philanthropic organizations, and we had the opportunity to meet and support many other families in our community. It was a time of learning for both of us, as we came to understand other families' experiences with deafness while sharing our own. Christopher was the star of the show, while I suddenly became Christopher's accomplice, taking on the role of Christopher's dad as opposed to Christopher being Tom Caulfield's son.

---▼---

After Christopher's graduation from St. Joseph's, our family had a new focus. Christopher had already accumulated an amazing one thousand hours of speech therapy, and my wife and I felt pretty good about his progress. Our goal now was for Christopher to complete another five hundred hours of therapy over the next three years. Our rationale was that the intensive speech therapy would continue to prime Christopher's brain to accept hearing and he would most effectively learn to verbally communicate.

The infamous first day of kindergarten came. Jen and I took Christopher to his new school and prepared to say good-bye. As we watched the other parents, it became clear that many of these children were entering a school classroom for the first time. Our parochial school was ready for that challenge. They had the parents and kids all meet in the school dining area together. We could see from the nonverbals of some parents and children that this was not going to be any easy transition.

After some general welcoming remarks from the head teacher, the announcement was made that it was time to part company. The emotions were palpable and some were simply agonizing. One student seemed pretty calm but as his parents led him to the room he suddenly raised his arms up like airplane's wings and would not go through the door. The mom just broke down and left. The dad and teacher remained and used barely enough leverage to get the boy's hyperextended body through the doorway. And with that, the dad too departed. As we looked at Christopher and he looked back at us, we had this sense of, "wow, been there, done that." After all, Christopher had been to preschool and had already made these adjustments. So it was smooth: in walked Christopher and out we went.

At the end of his first day, Jen and I picked him up for the short drive home. With much anxiety I asked the big question. "How did things go in school today, Christopher?" Jen and I waited nervously for his response.

"Okay," he said. Candidly, we were so concerned about him missing things or kids not talking to him because he was Deaf, we did not know what to say next. Before we could even consider another question, Christopher followed up with, "It was easy. All they do is play."

When I heard this my heart dropped. I thought, "We have had Christopher for so many years doing regimented therapy, he actually may not understand the concept of play!" So I smiled politely and held to my faith that this too would be an evolving process.

We were so very excited for Christopher's new beginning with kindergarten. After all of the work our whole family had put in, and especially Christopher, we were elated to have made it this far.

An unsung hero in our journey was Christopher's sister, Rachel. Rare was the day when she objected to the extra attention he would receive. In her most altruistic way, she welcomed all the challenges we were facing with Christopher. If that meant assisting with those relentless at-home speech therapy sessions, she did it effortlessly. She also was Christopher's constant companion, both around the house and when we were out and about. Even now, her strength and selflessness continue to blow me away.

As we entered into a relationship with Christopher's new parochial grade school, we recognized we might have some additional challenges. One issue was that the school was old and not as acoustically conducive to Christopher's hearing as we would have liked. However, some of the teachers were very strict and didn't tolerate a lot of ambient noise or loud conversations in their classrooms, which was great for Christopher. In addition, the school's leadership had created a caring religious environment in which the students would learn compassion and respect for one another.

We felt we could manage the challenges of the physical environment at the new school, but Christopher's reading level presented a different kind of challenge. Our instincts told us he was behind in reading when compared to his peers, and thus would need additional help in this area. We had spent so much time prior to this working on his speech and listening skills, we frankly didn't focus enough on reading. However, we had somewhat of an ace in the hole waiting to help out. Once again Rachel was more than up to the challenge to jump-start her brother on the path to reading better. Rachel was reading at a level three grades ahead of her classmates. That plus some unbelievable patience on her part reminded me of a combine going through a cornfield in the Midwest during harvest season as she worked for hours with Christopher. So there we were surrounding Christopher with every resource we had to help him be the best he could be. Our family actually probably would have been bored without all these goals!

———▼———

I grew up playing sports, and basketball had been my favorite. Christopher, however, was drawn to the sport of football from a very early age—even before he started kindergarten. I dreaded the inevitable conversation where I would have to tell him that playing football, even while wearing a helmet, could cause injury to his cranium and directly impact his implant. By the time he was six years old, many of his peers had begun trying out for Pee Wee football and I knew I couldn't avoid the topic forever.

The day of the "talk" came when he and I were pretending to run football plays in our rec room. "Christopher, you know football is really rough and Grandpa would not

let any of us play," I blurted. He looked at me with kind of a sad look. "It wasn't a mean thing," I quickly added, "he just didn't want us to get injured in a way that when we grew up it would be hard to walk around without hurting."

Christopher's eyes narrowed. "If you get hurt, what happens next?"

I responded, "You can't play for a while and sometimes you may need surgery." I then explained the inherent dangers of the game to Christopher, but I also let him know that the field-goal kicker position might be something he could safely try. Shortly thereafter, I found myself in the backyard erecting a PVC-type pole set into small-scale football goalposts. I figured it would give him something to do

Christopher starting grade school

while his friends were at practice. As it turned out, when Christopher wasn't kicking the ball with me, he was out in that backyard playing by himself. That meant he was doing a lot of kicking and retrieving. To make things easier on himself, he positioned the goalposts in front of a small hill in our backyard. If his kick went as planned, the ball would pass the uprights, hit the hill, and roll right back to him. His tenacity was endless. All those past speech therapy repetitions had apparently given him the strong will to work hard.

Having to tell Christopher which activities he could and could not participate in, given his deafness, had been heartbreaking for me. I wished Christopher could do anything he wanted to, but individuals with cochlear implants just plain can't do certain things safely. I knew I would never be able to forgive myself if Christopher were to be hurt even more by playing football, so for his own well-being, I canceled his football endeavor and the dream that went along with it. It was difficult for me not to feel horrible about what couldn't be.

Christopher eventually elected to play soccer, mainly because he had seen his sister give it a try. During one of his early first-grade games, he somehow corralled a free ball that had squirted out of the beehive of kids as it moved down the field. From there, he dribbled that ball up about twenty feet away from the goal and angled down on it like a laser beam. Like any proud dad, I stood waiting to watch our son score his first soccer goal. Time stopped as he drew his leg back and let her rip. That soccer ball, just like the many footballs in our backyard, cleared the upright over the goalie's head by at least seven feet. As a field goal it may have been good, but no one cheered "gooooaal" after that kick. Instead, a teammate had to chase the ball down to a stream that was twenty yards away.

I wished the soccer kids had shown a similar fortitude with Christopher as they had in practicing their soccer skills. But life is funny, and Christopher found his niche anyway. He had learned from the start that soccer is an international game, and at times his teammates had resembled a United Nations team. Although he struggled to befriend some of the kids on his team, Christopher easily connected with the young boys from Nigeria, Germany, and India. It seemed to Jen and me that he shared something in common with those first-generation American students: they were all still somewhat struggling to master the English language. Luckily for us, the international kids embraced the Deaf kid, and a special group emerged. Our family suddenly had a new diverse group of friends whom we cherished. An interesting by-product of Christopher's new relationships was that his international friends averaged one to two years ahead of their peers in soccer ability. Put candidly, they knew the World Cup before they had even attended preschool.

I thought it was spectacular that the international boys Christopher had met through soccer had started learning two languages before the age of five. However, they were difficult speech models for our son to learn from. We were looking for friends who talked slowly, loudly, and repetitively. Other boys could be loud, but they rarely talked slowly or had an interest in repeating themselves. For now we were grateful Christopher had been welcomed into the circle of such a friendly group of boys.

―――――▼―――――

As Christopher entered the second grade, we were quite comfortable with his language skill set, and we were becoming more at ease with his listening skills too. Of course we still had to deal with the normal difficulties that stemmed from Christopher's inability to listen well in larger groups. We found it was much better for him to have just one buddy over to play than for him to have two or three friends at our place at the same time. Inevitably, a large group of friends together created conversations that moved too quickly for Christopher to follow. This caused him to feel embarrassed and isolated, and it eventually led him to withdraw. As with many things, it took some trial and error before we figured out what worked best.

Overall, Jen and I were learning to get through many difficult issues as parents. Once Christopher successfully mastered one developmental phase, we would quickly arrange for him to take on something new. And there was always something new. With his listening skills on track, we turned our attention back to his reading. We anticipated this might be a struggle for him. Most hearing individuals learn to read phonetically— relating each letter to a different sound. Because Christopher's hearing had been com-

Christopher in soccer

promised since infancy, for him, learning to read would require a more creative approach. He specifically had issues with select vowels and consonants. For example, Christopher was unable to hear the V sound. With that being the case, he had to construct a visual image for all words containing the V sound. It was a complicated and slow process that made learning to read a lot less fun.

Since most of his vowel enunciation was pretty good, he had scored okay on his first-grade reading test at his parochial school, and to our surprise, the school did not place him in a special reading class. For us, being around other kids and knowing our daughter's ability in reading at this age led my wife and me to be concerned about the test's validity. We felt we had not spent enough focus on reading prior to this for us to find ourselves in the average range. So we sought out a private professional reading institute on our college campus to evaluate Christopher and offer us a second opinion. We knew that this group would be able to determine Christopher's level via their more comprehensive assessment. From this more in-depth analysis, we learned that Christopher was in fact a year behind his reading peers.

Now we had a new decision to make. Christopher's school had limited resources, so further study would have to come from us. Rachel in particular had really worked diligently to get Christopher where he was with reading, but she could only take him so far. Should we attempt additional tutoring on our own or hire an outside tutor? We asked other professionals for recommendations and learned that the private agencies were good at teaching reading to children with hearing loss. Although it would be expensive, we couldn't be more certain of the results. So Jen and I financially bit the bullet and enrolled Christopher in a special reading institute for the summer between second and third grade.

As the tutoring continued, I could see that Christopher's success would depend on his not getting frustrated. With emotional coaching for Christopher, the tutor was able to effectively teach him essential reading strategies. I would have to say that the intentional stop at the local ice cream shop after a successful session went a long way as well toward his reading improvement.

That same summer, Jen and I couldn't help but notice Christopher's size. As we had learned from our experience with Rachel, this was the age when the girls typically outgrew the boys in height. Christopher, however, was by far the tallest child in his class, whether boys or girls.

This height difference was most pronounced on the athletic field, where Christopher excelled. As he began participating in Little League and park district sports, we discovered that his height led others to respect him. Christopher's youth coaches also really seemed to love working with him, and from our view, who wouldn't? Christopher had been dissed enough for his disability in the past that to make up for it, he worked very hard to be the best athlete he could be. He could run fast, and he also had a refined sense of vision and kinesthetic awareness, meaning he knew how to move his body exactly the way he wanted it. These talents allowed him to be successful in sports such as soccer, baseball, and basketball. Further, he was always the kid who helped the other players up if they were knocked down while playing. Both his teammates and his opponents felt he was a great sport to be around. All in all, Jen and I thought he was simply a joy to watch.

Since the time Christopher was very young, Jen and I had made sure he actively participated in sports. One reason was that he had a natural ability for it and we wanted to encourage development of his God-given talents. Another reason, also important to us, was the social aspect of playing sports. Like many other parents, we fretted almost daily about whether Christopher would fit in with his peers. His deafness only added to our angst. It has been very well documented that Deaf kids can suffer serious bouts of loneliness and alienation. Knowing this, we pushed sports as a place where Christopher could also learn to navigate relationships with the other kids. While this strategy worked for one-on-one interactions, Christopher continued to struggle with group get-togethers.

At one of his postseason Pee Wee Little League parties, the struggle was on full display. The boys there were jovial and rowdy, and one could easily see why our son was left out. He was simply unable to handle all of the simultaneous talking. Most often Jen and I would actively recruit the congenial kids, who talked slowly and sometimes loudly, for Christopher to talk to at these parties. These were the same kids we chose to have play dates with Christopher. This worked well, but nothing pulled at our heartstrings more than watching a half dozen seven- and eight-year-olds laughing and joking together while our son desperately tried to have a good time even though he couldn't hear the conversation.

Christopher had the opportunity to try out many different summer camps during his early grade school years. His parochial grade school had been a very affirming environment in which the fear of God's wrath had probably caused many of the kids in his school to be civil. Summer camps, we knew, could be a much different environment, but we believed Christopher would benefit from being around a diverse group of boys. We first experimented with enrolling Christopher in a sports fitness camp when he was eight years old. This went well because Christopher really liked the athletic staff and there was such a variety of activities over the summer at the camp. We felt it was a great first step. The summer reading camp we signed him up for was a different story. After a few sessions, Jen and I had a talk about how it was going.

"Do you think we should keep sending him?" she asked. "He doesn't seem to enjoy it at all. I wonder if it's really worth it."

I had to agree that it was not as positive of an experience for him as some of the other camps he had attended. "He is working extra hard at something he isn't a natural at," I said. "I don't think we can blame him for not liking it as much as the sports camps."

After more discussion, we opted to keep him enrolled in the camp because we knew it would ultimately be good for his academic development.

Christopher's favorite camps were sports related, however, and over time we immersed ourselves in these. One summer, our family hosted a top-flight soccer camp counselor who was visiting from Britain for a one-week camp. Christopher thrived on his one-on-one experiences with the young, energetic counselor. Their relationship extended beyond the day camp to the backyard after dinner, where Christopher learned additional soccer skills. Our son was in awe of the twenty-year-old college player from overseas. As parents, we too marveled at the counselor's exceptional athletic ability. One day he asked Jen if there was a nearby fitness center where he could work out. "Of course," she said. "The one I go to is about two miles down the road. I can give you a lift if you'd like." Our British counselor graciously turned down her ride offer but accepted her guest pass. From there, he ran down to the fitness center and worked out for well over an hour before running back to our house. Mind you, this was all after he had put in a full eight-hour day in ninety-degree weather with soccer campers. Now that is commitment!

At the end of the week, the day came for our new British friend to depart. He gathered his bags in our front room and readied himself for the ride to the airport. Transitions were always difficult for Christopher, and Jen and I saw that our boy was going to greatly miss his new hero who had come from across the Atlantic where he lived down the road from the royal family. We all bid our most fond farewells to a really great young man who had befriended our son in a very special way that summer.

Ah, but there were always new transitions. Later that year, our family was in the process of building a new house. We had sold our old house, which Christopher had fondly named the Yellow House because of its exterior color, and planned to move to a townhouse while the new house was under construction. The good news was that the new home was only a mile down the road in the next subdivision over. The bad news was that Christopher, at age eight, was awfully fond of our current house and did not want to move. I learned that most clearly when we informed him that a newly married couple had just bought our Yellow House. He burst into tears at the news. Desperate to calm him, I pulled out the glossy pictures and floor plan of our new house. "Look, Christopher. See this room here? That's what you call a rec room. We're going to have one in our new basement." He started to calm down but I wasn't sure it would last. That's when I started promising him stuff we could put in there that I hoped we could afford. By the end of the conversation I think he was more distracted than soothed, and we moved on.

Admittedly Christopher had every right to be nostalgic about the Yellow House. He had learned a great deal in the years we lived there. He had discovered his speech there, which had to have been huge for a Deaf kid. Both his first pets, a cat and a dog, had been buried in the yard. He had also learned how to play basketball and kick a football and soccer ball there. No wonder it took some considerable effort on our part to finally convince him it was okay to move on. While we camped out in the townhouse, I periodically took both kids over to the construction site so they could see how their new place, which Christopher affectionately named the Red House, was coming along.

That summer concluded with our family having a great time visiting relatives in California. Given some videos to watch along the way, Christopher and his sister were fantastic travelers. This trip, in particular, was a visual extravaganza for us all. We saw the Oklahoma City National Memorial, the Grand Canyon, some San Diego dolphins in the wild, the redwoods in Marin County, and even the "rock," Alcatraz. Our travels were a way for our family to find comfort through the stressful times of working with Christopher, so he could become the best he could be.

CHAPTER 4

ORGANIZED HOOPS, HERE WE COME

---▼---

A s the new school year began, life was becoming fairly stable for Christopher. His speech was quite good, and when he wore his hair longer, thereby covering the implant, many people didn't even know he was Deaf. Reading still was our nemesis, however, and we made it our family's mission—with Rachel the bookworm leading the way—to help Christopher grow in this area.

On the technology front, his biomedical devices were performing admirably. One of our biggest fears was if for some reason we had a technology failure. We knew the external speech processor—a black box about the size, durability, and weight of a handheld calculator that he wore on his belt—could be replaced if needed. The speech processor received sounds from the microphone on Christopher's head, and in a millisecond it would transmit those sounds as impulses back into Christopher's brain via the auditory nerve at the base of the cochlea. Without it, the implant would be useless. In case of emergencies, we had a program already set up at our medical clinic where all the external processor's settings were defined and stored if anything needed to be fixed or replaced.

For as cautious as we were with the external components, the internal device just underneath his skin above his left ear we safeguarded even more intently. It had been surgically implanted in a long and complex procedure that resulted in unfortunate partial paralysis to portions of the left side of his face. Needless to say, we never wanted to have to go in and replace the internal device.

The cochlear implant had made such a difference in Christopher's schooling. Fourth grade had been kind of a last hurrah for him at his parochial school, and he moved quickly on to fifth grade. I had great apprehension about what fifth grade would bring. There would be no more S's or S-pluses. He would be given the real grades, and my hope was that he would be in the best letter range possible. The implant, along with all our hard work, had made that dream possible.

Fifth grade also marked Christopher's first year of organized basketball. In my heart, I knew he really wanted me to volunteer as a coach at his school, but I had been his teacher in the driveway and at the recreation center. I wanted a less-biased person to coach him going forward.

Christopher was nearly five feet two inches tall now, and my wife and I hoped this first year in uniform would be an enjoyable experience for him. It was something new, though, and the loud gyms crammed with yelling and screaming fans were not ideal for the Deaf kid. We agreed to reserve judgment and just see how the season went.

To our surprise, Christopher's November practices began with relentless training and fundamental sessions with his new coach. Christopher was such a natural athlete he seemed unaffected by the training regimen. However, as a former player and coach myself, I was immediately concerned about this style of coaching. It seemed that Christopher's coach was deviating from the mission of fifth-grade basketball as stated in the school handbook. Essentially, the handbook said the fifth-grade coach's goal was to promote team play. His job was not to have his team win at all costs.

By the time December came, we could see the coach had already selected eight boys to be his "players." I suppose I should have been flattered that he had chosen Christopher to be a part of his group, but I believed the coach was disenfranchising the remaining boys on the team. I decided meeting with the coach and expressing my concerns was the right thing for me to do. Picking up Christopher one day, I asked the coach if there was a time when we could talk. "I'd like to meet with you later in the week if your schedule permits," I said.

He was very friendly and essentially said, "Sure, anytime after practice."

The very next day I stopped in to talk with him. We both took a seat on the bleachers looking out at the court. I did my best to lay out my concerns without offending him in any way. I learned pretty quickly that he was a man of few words and had very strong ideas on his ways of coaching. When I had said what I wanted to say, the coach responded with, "I can tell who is going to be a player by the way he runs." He also claimed that the boys who were not playing were not tough enough. I walked away from our meeting having a better understanding of why some of the coach's former players and their parents had given him the nickname of Drill Sergeant, or DS for short.

The team started off with a victory against another Christian school in the area. Unfortunately, it was a shallow victory, since our coach had previously remarked that our team's win would be guaranteed. He also continued to mainly play only the eight players he had identified as serious contenders. DS's coaching technique initiated a problem for our team's eager fifth graders who were all interested in having playing time. Little did I and the other parents realize, but the "athletic pollution" we all feared was suddenly in the waters.

DS trained the boys like they were pit bulls. This caused the new players, who were not yet in good physical condition, to quit the team. Whenever our team lost a game, DS yelled at the players in the locker room. This and other behavior led a number of boys to either lose interest in the game or have low confidence. By midseason, a group of very concerned parents began to stay and watch the basketball practices. In all my years of having played and coached basketball, I had never witnessed a time when parents actively sat through a two-hour-long practice in order to ensure that their kids were not being verbally harmed. The more I contemplated it, the more I believed the parents needed to confront DS about his actions. I also knew I needed to be honest with Christopher about DS's unacceptable behavior. In February, the parents finally took their concerns to the school principal, but to no avail. The principal appeared to bury her head in the sand with the situation and no response was what the parent group was left to deal with.

The issue came to a head one day when I observed Christopher struggling in practice. He ran a play a different way than DS liked, so DS stopped the practice. DS, in his own way, then explained to Christopher how to correctly run the play. I heard Christopher respond, "Oh," to him in affirmation, and the play resumed. I thought maybe I had prejudged DS's coaching ability a little too harshly, as he had handled that situation very well. Then Christopher ran another sequence in a way that didn't work for DS, and the coach again shut down the play. Then we heard DS say to Christopher, "Listen, 'Oh,' if you can't get it right, you will need to sit down and watch." Intimidated, Christopher turned silent. Those of us in the stands were stunned. One parent even came over to me and apologized for Christopher's humiliation. I could see from the mist in the parent's eye that he understood how difficult it was for a Deaf child, or any child with a disability, to affirmatively say that he or she understood something during a confusing situation. Unfortunately, DS had labeled Christopher with a new name, "Oh." At that moment, I knew DS and I would need to meet again.

Before I had a chance to set up a meeting with DS, however, another incident occurred at practice that same week. DS was in the process of subbing Christopher into a half-court offense, but when he called Christopher to go in, Christopher was too far away to hear him. DS became frustrated and put another player out on the court. It was sad for me to watch my son walk up to his coach for clarification only to be told, "Never mind."

To a certain extent we were between a rock and a hard place. DS had volunteered his time away from his business job in the community to coach his son's team. He only came to the school for sports a few times a week. The school, therefore, had only a loose supervisory role with his coaching. That left a lot of the negotiating to the parents. So off to round number two I went, asking Christopher's coach if we could meet again after practice.

The day of my second meeting with DS finally came. As it turned out, the meeting was once again quick and to the point. I instructed DS to call my son by his real name and to stop addressing him with belittling terms such as "Oh." I also let him know that he couldn't selectively substitute the hearing players into the game just because the Deaf player didn't hear his voice. DS, while clearly not liking the feedback, took it. I was pretty confident that he knew based on recent player attrition that Christopher could be next to move along to a more affirming activity. DS did change his attitude toward Christopher, but his general coaching philosophy did not budge.

Overall, that year's basketball season was rough, and most of the parents were calling for DS's removal as coach by the end of the season. I wondered how the school would respond given that about two out of every three parents wanted him gone.

During the off-season that year, the principal and booster club sent out an athletics survey to the parents asking about each student athlete's experience in school sports. Parents on Christopher's team responded to the survey with an outpouring of complaints. There were even some drawings, pictures, and a basketball team narration regarding our players' unfortunate experiences with DS. The survey resulted in the school not inviting DS to coach again the following year and many of the fifth-grade basketball boys and their parents expressed huge relief.

———◆———

Christopher's experience with DS did not change his love for the game. Christopher had turned enough heads in the gym that shortly after the end of the season, he received an invitation to try out for the Boys and Girls Club travel basketball team in our city. Although he was only in fifth grade, he would be trying out for the sixth-grade team. We soon discovered it was a darn good program too. The sixth-grade team had won its division in the previous year's national championship. The kids on this team played at an entirely different level than the kids on Christopher's parochial school team.

The Boys and Girls Club, which was only about a half mile from Christopher's grade school, was a safe and secure place for the youth of our inner city. The staff was extremely congenial to Christopher. The basketball facility was actually a converted church. The floors were not wood but rather a rubberized tile placed square after square to become a court. The hoops were bent as if people had been hanging on those rims excessively. But in the end, it didn't matter.

When we arrived for the tryout it was clear the other boys invited had been warming up for a while already. Their shirts were drenched with sweat to the point that indvidual players' shorts were starting to get saturated as well. With these boys being about in the sixth grade, that intensity was unusual. I had a feeling we were in for an education.

The tryout began with a series of endurance runs that lasted about five minutes. Christopher finished in great shape on these and I thought, "Wow, things are starting off well." Next came the suicides—quick sprints back and forth within the gym lines. This went on for about fifteen minutes with very few breaks. Christopher was still keeping up, but he was definitely in the middle range, not leading the pack. From there the boys did shooting drills off the dribble as well as in place, competed in free-throw contests, and went through a series of tests to measure true vertical jump.

At the end of the tryout, I asked Christopher how he thought he had done.

"I can't really tell," he said. "At first I felt good but it was really hard. Harder than I expected." He added that this kind of play was "totally different." He said these guys were not only "very fast but strong and played much higher up toward the hoop."

It was obvious he would need to be more physical and rebound better if he wanted to play with these boys. Forget that: These players were clearly not boys. They were young men. On the other hand, Christopher's shooting was probably the best on the team.

I offered him some encouragement. "I noticed sometimes when you were shooting, all the players were in 'check it out' mode. I could also tell the coach admired your shooting ability."

"I just hope I did well enough to make the team," he said.

About a week later, we got the call. Christopher had made the team! I was overwhelmed with pride when I heard the news.

The practices were heavy on the running, but Christopher was used to that after his parochial school team training. His new coach, Kharis Gordon, was relentless about the players taking the ball to the goal. He explained that this was the best way for them to finish strong. Coach Gordon also didn't call any fouls, so those boys learned how to finish to the basket with power. At first this strategy blew Christopher away. How could anyone not call this type of contact a foul? However, as time went on, Christopher learned to stop expecting the call. I also found myself looking less at the contact and more at how Christopher would finish. It was definitely a new day and we admired Coach Gordon and the affirming nature he had with all the players. It might seem trivial but he was continuously asking open-ended questions to the young men before and after practice. The players in turn were drawn to this unconditional acceptance. Heck, you could tell right off it didn't matter to Coach Gordon what you were struggling with, as he met you in a real conversation based on respect.

For years our family had avoided the travel soccer teams because of the time involved and the seriousness of the play at such a young age. The time commitment was still an issue, but Christopher was older now and ready to get a little more serious about basketball. In addition, this travel team was a tremendous opportunity for Christopher to experience diversity. At practices he was easily spotted as the lone white kid on the court, and I liked the fact that this team was racially the polar opposite of his parochial school's squad.

In March, the practices with his new team began in preparation for the games later that month. Christopher and I were both excited for the games to begin. And, wow, they were so very fast paced, and I thought the level of play was two times more difficult than the parochial team's play. When compared to the park district, it was probably four times as difficult. I questioned whether Christopher could ever go back to the good old days of park district play after this. In my heart I hoped he could return to play there since the park district team had been great for Christopher socially, but somehow I knew it was unlikely.

Christopher probably played thirty games over the course of the spring and summer, and the travel wasn't too bad. He and I always drove together in our hybrid, since those fifteen-passenger vans were frankly a bit average in their rollover safety rating. They were also way too loud for Christopher to hear anything the players said to him. For me, it was great bonding time with my son.

By July, Christopher's team was winning most of their games. When the team did get outscored by an opponent, it was usually due to our players emotionally imploding. Christopher was shocked to witness some of the better players on the travel team experiencing meltdowns. The unbelievable example of this occurred in one of our early tough games, which we were actually playing at home. One of our players was bringing the ball up court. Once he was over the half-court line he got caught in a trap by the opposing team's defenders. With nowhere to go and wedged by the right angle of the midcourt and sideline, he began to get extremely frustrated. With the five-second held-ball call looming, he did the unfathomable. With just one quick thrust of his neck, our player head-butted the opposing player in the trap and knocked him on his back to the floor. It was like a knock-out punch in boxing but instead of using his fist, our player had used his head. The referee, instead of calling the five-second call, whistled a foul on our player. Coach Gordon reacted in a nanosecond by calling a timeout. He sent in a substitute to try to defuse the volatile situation and, thankfully, it worked.

While that episode was fairly well contained, in other instances a few players on our team appeared ready to fight as soon as things didn't go well for them on the floor. This became a real embarrassment for the team on several occasions. My hope was that the situation would be resolved before the team potentially played in a national tournament.

That July, after months of hard work, playing in the national tournament became a reality, and Christopher's travel team was headed to Fort Wayne, Indiana. Jen stayed home with Rachel while Christopher and I road-tripped to the Hoosier state.

The gym in Fort Wayne was a shrine to Indiana basketball over in Bloomington. There were eight full-sized basketball courts and tons of sports memorabilia displayed in glass cases. It isn't every day that one is surrounded by NBA players' jerseys and Bobby Plump's sneakers from the movie *Hoosiers*. It was obvious that Fort Wayne was the place to be for youth basketball that July.

Our boys appeared a little nervous when they first took the floor at nationals, and it affected their play. After some discussion with their coach, they got it together and began playing up to their potential. At this level, however, everybody was great. After the first day and a half, we were four and two, but all the games were decided by five points or less. The boys would have to stay in the moment and keep getting the wins if they wanted to go far in the tournament.

The play on the court was tough, but it was the horseplay back at the hotel on the second night that became the real story of the tournament. Christopher and I always roomed together, since he couldn't hear a fire alarm when sleeping without his implant. Although at times it made it difficult for him to bond with other teammates, that night our sleeping arrangement turned out to be a good thing. Some of the boys on the team decided to break their curfew and visit an adjacent hotel, where the female players were staying. The next morning, after Christopher and I came down to breakfast, everything hit the fan. I learned the manager had told our coach he was kicking our team out of the hotel.

I didn't have the heart to tell Christopher that we might have to leave the hotel due to a few players' inappropriate actions the night before. At that point, I thought our Boys and Girls Club leaders would undoubtedly become involved and tell us to come home. The kids' chance at a title would be over. It all couldn't have come at a worse time, either. Our team had just started to get the hang of the tournament. We had been playing some good basketball against some of the best teams from Ohio, Michigan, and Indiana. Before the final verdict was in, Coach Gordon met with more of the hotel management folks to see what he could do. Believe it or not, he worked his magic and they agreed to let us stay! The only condition was that our boys had to agree to an early curfew with lights out during the remainder of our visit. The boys honored their commitment.

Now that we were back on track with our lodging, the players could focus on playing good basketball. The going would be tough from then on out, since our team had won the previous year's championship. During the final two days of the tournament, it was clear that ours was the best Illinois team on the court. Our boys had out-hustled those pesky Michigan and Indiana teams to eliminate them from the tournament. Unfortunately, the Ohio team was another story. The Ohio players were just too big and strong for our spindly guys, Christopher included. In the end, it wasn't bad finishing as one of the final eight teams in the tournament, and it had also been a fun father-and-son trip for the two of us. Christopher and I said our good-byes to Fort Wayne, Indiana. We would surely always remember the basketball shrine there and playing in the state that seemed to have invented basketball.

Back in our home city, the basketball news didn't end. My wife and I were contacted by a parent member of our booster club who confirmed what we already knew. DS was no longer the coach at our parochial school, and a new coach had been selected to take his place. Obviously, the parent and student complaints, as well as the survey responses, had led to the change. In a way, I wasn't surprised by the news. The diocese was nationally focused on preventing any abusive situations involving its clergy, teachers, or volunteers in the schools. In my mind, all school workers and volunteers needed to create a safe environment for the children. Christopher was all right with his school's decision. He had witnessed firsthand DS intimidating his fellow teammates, along with the belittling behavior he had shown him as well. Many of the boys on the team, however, also felt sorry for DS's son, who remained on the squad.

———•———

Christopher's sixth-grade year began similarly to his previous ones. Soccer was in full swing, and it was always fun for Christopher. Athletically, he once again demonstrated that he had stayed in shape throughout the year. An unexpected problem, however, was creeping up. After watching some of his practices, I began to wonder whether Christopher was becoming too tall to play soccer within his age group. He ran very well, without a doubt, but the smaller boys exhibited a quickness and tenacity that, at times, made it more difficult for Christopher to keep up during the matches. By the end of the season, I suspected soccer would soon be falling off the radar for Christopher.

Basketball began before soccer ended, which meant that Christopher was involved in two sports for about two weeks in midfall. His new basketball coach was great and very dedicated to helping the players. More special yet, Coach Thompson gave all the parents who attended a team meeting his assurance that he would treat all of the boys on his team respectfully. This immediately relieved the parents from having to attend practices. Another positive was that the coach had no son on the team, so there wouldn't be an opportunity for bias.

But it wasn't all good news. Our new coach appealed to the parents for help coaching the team. He needed an assistant or two to help with the boys, since the squad was too large for one person to handle. Given the work schedules of most of the parents, there were no takers. Without an alternative, the new coach brought DS back as an assistant. The parent group met informally to discuss the new development, but we were forced to concede to the new coach, since he was the one in charge and we were not able to step up when he had asked for help. Our hope as parents was that DS would follow Coach Thompson's instructions. Besides the negative feelings from last season, I had strong opinions about parents who coached teams that their own children were on. There

Ten years old

was just too much potential for bias, which could cause conflict among the rest of the players on the team.

By midseason, our worries appeared to be for naught. The new basketball season was dramatically different from the year before. Coach Thompson had heard the parents' voices, and he understood that our goal was not for our children to win the World Cup in sixth grade. As parents, we were overjoyed that the new coach was committed to allowing each player on the team the opportunity to improve his play. This even included the boys with little basketball experience. Gone was the year of select players getting the most playing time. All of Coach Thompson's players mattered to him.

Unbelievably, Christopher had been a no-show at his first basketball practice with the new coach. His parochial school was academically rigorous, and Christopher had suddenly found himself ineligible to play. The school's grading scale was tough, with an 85 percent to 93 percent being a B, and a 94 percent to 100 percent being an A. According to the school policy, students who fell into the D range—70 percent to 78 percent—would be ineligible to play until their grade rose to a C or above. Christopher's nemesis at the time was social studies. The class came equipped with a new teacher who had expectations and then some. As of the first practice, there had been only one quiz in her class and Christopher had not done well. With no other grades to counterbalance the poor quiz result, he was off the team. That didn't last long, though. The very next day, Christopher had another graded assignment that he did extremely well on. The teacher recalculated the grades in the class and Christopher was back in business for practice on day two. Fortunately, Christopher quickly learned what he needed to do to bring his best to that classroom, and he ended the quarter with an A in social studies.

Basketball went fairly smoothly throughout the rest of the season even though the parent group noticed that Coach Thompson had given DS more and more direct coaching responsibilities as time progressed. In the end, our team won a holiday tournament and finished with a winning season. Following the last game of the tournament, DS gave the locker-room speech to the team. That's when things fell apart once again. According to some of the players, DS, with less than eloquent oratory style, announced that this would be the last year every player on the team would play. "Only the best players will get playing time next season," the boys said. I remember that day vividly. The players did not come bouncing out of the locker room with the typical elation you would expect after concluding a winning season. It was more like they had had a nice airplane ride all year and right at the end, they missed the landing strip. The parent group now feared the church and school had plans to forgive DS and allow him to be the head coach the following season. Thank goodness for the month of April and the beginning of Christopher's travel ball so our family could escape all the drama.

———◦———

Christopher's travel team tryouts were once again very competitive that spring. Christopher had played on the same sixth-grade team as a fifth grader, but that didn't mean we could assume he would make the squad again. Our family's hope was for Christopher to not only make the team but also get in some good playing time. Much to our relief, he earned a spot on the team for the second year in a row.

The new travel team season began with some terrible news. Coach Gordon, who had been with the team for many years, needed to step down for personal reasons. The director of the Boys and Girls Club quickly paid me a visit.

"Mr. Caulfield, here I am the leader of this club and I am without a coach. I have come to see if you know of anyone who would be interested in volunteering for the open coaching position."

I had a great deal of respect for the director, as both a leader and a social worker at the club. He was the first person who really reached out to Christopher in an affirming way when Christopher went to the club for a tour. I was motivated to help him and told him I would let him know if I came up with any names for him.

Before I had closed the door behind him, I was already going through a mental Rolodex of basketball dads. I knew one dad who would be good, but his job as a human resources officer left him with little spare time. I decided to discuss it with him anyway.

I arranged a time to speak to the dad and laid out the situation for him. "What do you say? Can you help us coach the team?" I asked.

"I'll do it, but only if you're head coach," he said. He added that he believed the boys on our team could really benefit from learning the importance of being good students as well as strong athletes. "I want you to teach the players the importance of academic excellence," he said. I was a little embarrassed and definitely flattered when he explained why he thought I was the right choice for the job. "Dr. Caulfield, you really get this," he said. "These boys need someone to genuinely pay attention to them and affirm them where they are at and give them the tools necessary to be successful in life, not just basketball."

I thought about the appropriateness of coaching my own son and weighed it against the fact that there would not be a team if I didn't volunteer to coach. I knew then I needed to step up and help.

We began our practices that April with a special emphasis on team. Unfortunately, I had witnessed a very talented squad self-destruct at times during the previous year's national tournament because the boys had played as individuals instead of as a team.

The team versus the individual model became most apparent during one particular practice. Our most athletic player drove very hard to the basket. Christopher, with help defense, cut the player off and blocked his shot. In response, the player threw the ball hard at Christopher, who displayed great reflexes and caught the ball. Mutual anger filled the air as both boys met chest to chest. I intervened, saying, "Anyone can block another player's shot." I was careful not to show favoritism toward my kid, who was just making a good basketball play.

Sadly, this particular boy didn't like that rationale. I knew him to be the same young player who, under a different coach, had continuously butted his way to the front of the three-man weave drill line so he could go as often as he desired. None of his coaches had ever confronted him before, presumably because they didn't want to lose his skill set on the court. Chest to chest with Christopher now, he had the look on his face that he would prefer to settle things physically and that would prove who was tougher. I separated the boys and when their heads had cooled somewhat, we got on with practice. Hours later, however, the player managed to get on the Boys and Girls Club public address system and broadcast mean things about Christopher across the club center. The young man was off the team in less than a week. Afterward, I explained what had happened to the rest of the team, and I could see the collective relief on the players' faces.

The boy's sudden departure from our team led me to think about the decision-making processes of these eleven- and twelve-year-olds. Did the other parents understand that this player's poor actions were what caused him to be removed from our team? Some parents probably thought that losing him would hurt us in nationals that year. But a destructive personality can cause more problems than talent alone can solve. My gut told me that building team chemistry would be the best way to compensate for the loss of such an athletic player.

Our practices continued with the usual drills to stress the fundamentals. We had lost most of our players from the year before, and this team had nowhere near the athletic ability of that elite eight team. Our first tournament was coming up soon, and I was noticeably uneasy about our readiness. There were three fifth graders and two sixth graders ready to go on our squad, but the remaining three or four players needed some help with their game. Given that, I knew we had our work cut out for us as a team.

Tournament play started in the east-central part of the state. We had practiced as much as we could, and the night before the tournament, I fell asleep feeling confident we were ready to give it our best.

We began the next day by outlasting the area home team, then outscored a good team from a large city near our home. With two wins in the books and just eight teams in the tournament, we had worked our way into the championship game. Our opponents were a squad from a small farm town outside of the tournament city. A local benefactor in the town had really wanted the group of rural boys to be successful. He donated his own money to build them a beautiful gym to use, and the boys had played together in it since their early grade school years. I knew this would be a good, tough game for us.

As usual, two or three die-hard families had traveled with us. Unfortunately, we were dwarfed by our opponent's following of about fifty fans in the stands. It was a tough game, as expected, but we were competitive. With less than thirty seconds left in the second half, the game was tied at forty-one. Christopher got the ball and hit a solid jump shot off a screen to put us in the lead. I wish I could say that our lead lasted. Instead, it went the opposing team's way for one more basket, sending the game into overtime. But the overtime was ours, and we ended up taking home first place in the tournament. I was elated, and our players were too. Our club hadn't won that tournament in two years.

Although I didn't know for sure, I believed Christopher was having a lot of fun in travel ball that year. All of the plays and defensive sets were now signaled via number or gesture, and I suspected that might play a role in his feeling more comfortable. I checked in with Christopher, who confirmed my suspicion. Life was good for the Deaf kid when he didn't have to struggle to hear in a loud gym.

———⚓———

The summer after sixth grade seemed like the perfect time to offer Christopher his fill of basketball camps. He had demonstrated he liked the game and frankly was very good for his age. However, I had some narrow parameters in mind.

"Christopher, I'm signing you up for basketball camp this summer."

"Okay. But you know I don't like the overnights." Given Christopher's deafness, he still had an aversion to staying in the provided housing when he attended camps. His main concern of course was that the staff might not be familiar with the emergency evacuation procedures for the disabled. "What would I do if there was a fire?" he asked.

"I know. That's why I narrowed the choices to camps closer to home. You can commute," I said.

We talked some more about his options, and after it was all said and done, Christopher was signed up for twelve weekly summer hoops camps. All the while, he would continue to play travel ball with the Boys and Girls Club team. Thankfully, our family hadn't scheduled any vacations that summer, since we were planning a Rose Bowl trip in January. I knew it would be a very busy summer, but I was happy to be Christopher's designated driver to and from all the camps.

Our first stop on the camp circuit was a small town just outside of our home's city limits. The town had a reputation for playing good basketball, and its school had even been home to a former NBA player. As I sat in the school complex, I marveled that an NBA player had come from this area. The school gym looked like something you would see at a high school four times its size. The camp was well run, and Christopher received his fair share of attention. The coach was impressed that Christopher, at his grade level, had the opportunity to attend numerous camps and experience varying players' talents. The word on the street was that this coach was strong, so I was happy to have Christopher learn from him. In fact, the coach was so strong that I had heard he was on the verge of being selected as a college-level assistant coach. This was all the more reason for Christopher to absorb as much as he could that week at camp.

Our next scheduled camp stop was at one of the many schools in our own city. Christopher had visited this school before and knew it well. The school's coaches were very assertive with Christopher. "Where are you planning to attend high school?" they would ask, even though high school was still two years away. Christopher had grown used to being asked this, however, and he always responded with, "I can tell you one thing. I'm not going to attend _____." He then inserted the name of the rival school in the blank. Many towns had school rivalries, and Christopher believed his camp coaches would be relieved to hear that he would not be on their rival school's roster after eighth grade. Whenever I heard him say this, I wondered from a Christian perspective if he was already being drawn into the politics of sports at such an early age.

The highlight of the camp week was the end of the session contests. I sat in the stands that day with a former Big Ten college player who was watching his own son compete. I observed as Christopher made nine out of ten shots from the free-throw line for his group of about fifteen seventh and eighth graders. Since Christopher was successful there, his next stop would be a shoot-off against a high school freshman to win a prize. Given that Christopher was three years younger, I wondered how it would play out. I had previously shared with Christopher that if he were to ever get into a shoot-off, he should attempt to put the pressure on the other kid. Unfortunately, his opponent was no kid. He had sideburns and a deep voice. Christopher quickly asked to shoot first, and I admired his assertiveness with his attempt to not have any pressure on himself. Jen and I had never been able to get him to assertively ask for any accommodations for his deafness, but this was different. This time there was hardware on the line. I watched as Christopher hit all five of his shots. The other young man hit four in a row, but his fifth shot rolled slightly off the rim. Several people clapped for the surprise finish. Christopher enjoyed his victory, and the two of us continued on our way through the camp circuit.

Our next stop was a nearby parochial high school. Christopher had already made his mark with the coach at this school too, since he had seen him play on his grade school team. That team was a feeder to the high school more often than not. This coach had appreciated Christopher's talent so much that he had invited him to work out with his freshman basketball team over the summer. The hardware story was the same at this camp as well. Christopher once again came home with one of the top camp awards. The shelf in Christopher's room was beginning to sag!

At the next camp, Christopher again found himself competing against a former college basketball player's son. I admit I thought Christopher had finally met his match, but to my surprise, he arrived home at the end of the week wearing not one but two medals.

A few weeks later, Christopher and I visited a university camp where he would be playing in the eight- to fourteen-year-old group. He was now twelve years old and would be comfortably in the middle of the age group. Although the camp was fifty miles away, we would not be staying overnight. Christopher still didn't feel it was safe. Thinking about this caused me considerable distress. Jen and I had been with Christopher every night since he was born. We realized he was scared to be in an unsupervised state that would make him vulnerable. As I reflected on this it just didn't seem fair at all. Candidly, due to his deafness, well, there was the "no football" talk because of the implant being potentially damaged inside his head. Can't ride in the noisy travel ball vans because he wouldn't be able to hear a thing once inside with all the simultaneous chatter. And now he can't have a fun residential experience at these out-of-town camps because of very real safety concerns. Instead, Christopher and I would drive an hour each way to the camp every day. While I regretted Christopher not being able to enjoy an overnight trip with his teammates, those camp commutes led to some great father-and-son time.

The university camp began with the usual formalities of dividing the players by grades and then having them meet the coaches. As Christopher lined up with the other twelve-year-olds, I noticed his seventh-grade friend stood a solid six feet two inches tall next to him. At five feet nine inches Christopher was considered to have pretty good height for his age, so the seventh grader in the line was really big! This boy also played travel ball. His size alone gave him potential.

At the end of the week, I was sitting in the mezzanine seating area of the university arena watching Christopher having fun shooting. This was completely normal for us. Since we had a bit of a drive home, we might as well take advantage of some court time after almost all the other campers had left for the day. As I was fascinated watching Christopher putting everything together on all the fundamentals we were working on with shooting, the Division I head coach at the school sat down with me. So there we were, two older men watching a grade schooler enjoy his time on the big-time court. Then the coach spoke. "We would like to invite Christopher to a fall basketball game here at the university," he said. I was stunned! "Fundamentally and athletically, Christopher had a super camp," he added. "It's quite exceptional that he is displaying that Larry Bird–type shot form at the seventh-grade level."

I regained my composure and gratefully accepted his offer for our family to attend a game in the fall. As he was talking, I felt he wasn't your typical coach in all sorts of ways. "Do you have children yourself?" I asked. He responded he did. "Do they play basketball? You know, given your occupation?" He replied that his kids were more into the "sports for life." Never having heard that phrase, I asked what those were. As easy as could be, he said, "Golf, swimming, and tennis," in that order.

Exactly two days later, I received a note from the coach's basketball office asking our family to choose a game that worked for our schedule. We were thrilled! It was our first contact by a Division I college coach, and Christopher had not even completed grade school yet.

From there, Christopher enrolled in a Big Ten school summer camp. Based on the scope of where most of the players came from, this camp had more of a midwestern draw. The camp format was pretty straightforward—work on drills and fundamentals part of the day and then play the tournament games. At this young age, tournaments were the main event where kids could play against others they had never met before and may never meet again. Unless, that is, they were lucky enough to advance to the highest level of tournament play with their school or perhaps with their travel ball team.

It was fun for me to watch a star-struck Christopher interacting with current and former college players. Who wouldn't have been star-struck? Three of the guys Christopher met up with at the camp had played on four straight high school state championship teams and at college NCAA tournament games. Even more interesting was the reciprocal admiration these superstar athletes had for Christopher. They seemed to instinctively understand how challenging it had been for Christopher to reach his current playing level while being Deaf.

On the last day, all the campers' parents came to town and watched the championship game alongside the coaches and the host school's college players. With just eight seconds left to go in the game, Christopher was fouled. As he lined up for the foul shot, I saw an assistant coach communicating with the host university's head coach. He pointed his finger at Christopher, raised his hand to his left temple, and appeared to be involved in a very detailed conversation. Meanwhile, Christopher's first free throw went in so clean you would have thought he had dropped it in from the ceiling.

I could see that the two coaches were keeping their eyes fixed on the Deaf kid. The head coach even stepped around another person to get a better look at Christopher, who was lining up for free throw number two. Christopher's second shot was money. The coaches took little notice. They appeared to be discussing what the device was on Christopher's head. The assistant coach pointed first to his own back and then to Christopher's lower back. I could tell he was describing Christopher's speech processor.

Back on the court, the game almost ended when the opposing team threw up a desperation shot. Christopher, however, was in a good position to get the rebound. With just one tick left on the clock and a two-point lead, Christopher was fouled again. He made quick work of his free throws, and his team won the camp championship.

Junior high basketball

After the game, the head coach from the Big Ten school came up to me to ask how the cochlear implant system worked, with the processor on the waist and the implant on Christopher's head. The coach shared that his own dad struggled with deafness, and I was happy to be able to tell our story and offer some understanding.

Christopher next attended a local community college camp, where he was initially grouped by age with the nine- to twelve-year-olds. After the first day of camp, however, the coach asked me if he could move Christopher to the thirteen- through sixteen-year-old group. Christopher and I were both flattered the coach had asked, but I was worried that the older, car-driving boys would hurt my son. As the camp continued, it was obvious that the much younger Christopher was not going to win any awards or gain any memorable moments this time around. Nevertheless, he had gained a great deal of experience while playing with the much better and more mature players.

This time in Christopher's life was enjoyable for me to witness. He had met so many new people, and his camp experiences had tremendously helped him with his social skills. Jen and I knew all too well that Christopher had not set any records for being invited to peer birthday parties, and we were actively trying to change that through each of Christopher's new social encounters.

Our busy summer with camps and competition with the Boys and Girls Club team ended that year with a trip to the final four for travel ball. Although Christopher's team did not advance further than that, it was still a special July. The boys on the team had worked so hard to reach their current level. With summer now winding down, Christopher was ready to make new memories playing junior high basketball.

CHAPTER 5

———————▼———————

Christopher began seventh grade at the same parochial school he had attended since kindergarten. We were thankful he did not have to switch schools the way so many public school students did. Transitions were always a challenge and we reveled in the rare break we had received.

Despite his height, Christopher played soccer again that fall. His intention was to stay in shape for basketball and to actively steer clear of DS, who was busy coaching the school's baseball team. While parent and student relations with DS were somewhat better, concerns about how the coach had treated the basketball boys remained. The parent group did not completely trust him. I, too, was very cautious. A part of me wanted to give DS the chance to improve, but another part of me understood just how vulnerable the self-esteem of Christopher and the other boys was during this stage in their lives. To say the least, a coach who rubbed a fair share of his players and their parents the wrong way created a difficult situation for the team.

It was too bad that Christopher had to dodge baseball just to avoid having DS as a coach. As a baseball player, Christopher had the reputation of having a live arm. In other words, he could naturally pitch with a high release point. At age thirteen, he was already in the ninety-ninth percentile for height, so his long arms could have been a real asset for the team.

Soccer was a different story. When I told Christopher's new coach that he was only in the seventh grade, her jaw dropped. She was sure he had to be an eighth grader. The coach's perspective of Christopher was further solidified when she saw the students perform some additional training runs. As she went over to meet with the team she began by gathering the boys together.

"Hello," she said. "I'm Julie and I will be your new coach this year."

With that brief introduction, she quickly got down to business and asked the team to warm up with two laps around the soccer field. Christopher stopped after one lap, and I signaled to him that he had one more lap to go. Darn! The Deaf kid's plight was that he either got the messages too late, or worse, he didn't get them at all. Frustrated, Christopher moved on at an even faster pace, lapping a few other players before finishing his second round-trip.

After the warm-up and some additional drills, Julie gathered the boys once again. "Tell me, why is Christopher always the first player to reach loose balls?" she asked. At first no one replied. Then I heard the boys joke under their breath, "Because he runs like Forrest Gump!" Christopher hadn't heard the hurtful comment, but I did. I guess it didn't really matter, though, since he was just there to play some soccer.

As time went on, it became apparent that Christopher, although younger than his teammates, was in far better shape. The coach, who was in incredible shape herself, took notice. She told the boys at great length that the team in the best shape has a considerable advantage in this sport. Just from her presence alone, looking like she walked right out of a soccer magazine, you could see these guys wanted to impress her. To build up the team's endurance, she asked all thirteen players to run to and from the goal lines in under thirty-five seconds. The boys quickly took off running like a bunch of kids heading for the water at the beach. Only one boy finished under thirty-five seconds. Guess who that was?

Julie now, sounding a bit frustrated while still trying to remain enthusiastic, said, "We are going again, and we all need to make it this time." The second try yielded the same result as the first. That was when the coach realized she had a bunch of joggers on her hands. She attempted the practice run three more times before she accepted that Christopher was the only boy who could finish in under thirty-five seconds.

Christopher's results led to a lightbulb moment for me. If he was really that fast, how would he do with cross-country running? To find out, Christopher and I made a visit to our local fitness center. We wanted to see how he would handle his first time on a treadmill. I noticed immediately the significant amount of noise he made while running. Those seventh-grade, size twelve sneakers sounded like water flippers on the rotating belt. Albeit a little noisily, Christopher quickly got the hang of it. Once he completed his warm-up, he started the timer and was off on a two-mile run. Time: twelve minutes and thirty-eight seconds. Not bad. Since I knew nothing about cross-country, however, I was left wondering how Christopher's time would compare to the other seventh-grade runners.

But first, priorities. It was now October, and the smell of basketball was in the air. Soccer wasn't over yet, but all the basketball families were gearing up. This new season came with DS attempting to convince the parent group that he was ready to try again. On the bright side, some parents claimed that DS had in fact mellowed. Christopher and I agreed to see if all this talk of him "mellowing" was true. We figured it had probably been pretty hard for DS to have been told that he couldn't coach the boys, and thus, he knew that he needed to change his ways. I guess Christopher wanted to see those changes for himself.

Christopher went into his first week of practice with an open mind. As a Christian, he sincerely wanted to give DS a second chance. Not long after practices had started, I asked him how it was going.

"I don't know. Coach seems to like what I'm doing," he said.

I secretly wondered if he really just liked Christopher's height. To make sure the coach and I were on the same page, I arranged to meet with DS at the school.

A few days later, as I waited for the meeting to start, I gazed around the cafeteria. Knowing how congested and loud it must be daily, I pictured Christopher attempting to hear his classmates talking to him. Christopher, I realized, most likely kept his head down and focused on eating rather than attempting to hear any conversation. I quickly snapped myself out of this reverie and refocused on the impending meeting.

DS arrived, and I took the lead. I told him, "It is critically important that you use signs and signals this year. It's the only way Christopher is going to be able to participate at his highest level." Christopher was coming into the year in the best shape of his life and still the tallest person in his grade. I knew DS wanted him to perform. "We are going to create some very noisy environments if we are a great team," I said. "We have to use signs on the court to make that happen."

DS agreed and indicated that he too wanted to develop more visual communication. With that, the meeting was over and we were on our way. I was pleased to see DS keep his word. He moved to quickly develop hand signals, and Christopher gained some respect for DS as a coach. At that point, Christopher and I made a pact to finish the season as long as DS continued to positively conduct himself.

Christopher's school year was off to a good start. Preseason practices weren't too rigorous for him, especially since he was just coming out of the soccer season. He also seemed to fit in a little better both at school and on the basketball team, and he appeared to have gained even more academic confidence during that first quarter.

The increased confidence was especially important to us. Since kindergarten Christopher had always sat in the front of the classroom because of his hearing loss. Still, he wasn't always able to catch everything the teacher said. To help, we purchased an FM system and microphone that enhanced his ability to hear the teacher in the classroom. Essentially the system brought the teacher's voice directly to Christopher's implant via the microphone. It was Christopher's responsibility then to exchange the microphone from teacher to teacher as he went to his various classes each day. We found the FM system to be particularly helpful when given to the keynote speaker at school assemblies. The range of the FM system was very powerful, which also led to some funny incidents. One day Christopher's teacher went to the washroom while the class was taking an exam. Christopher smiled as he worked on his test, the sound of a flushing toilet in the background. The great news was that Christopher's overall academic performance, including his reading skills, was steadily improving.

Christopher's first basketball game that season was at a parochial school in a small farming community south of town. His team hadn't played this school in sixth grade, but I recalled all too well how the opponent had outscored our fifth-grade team in this same gym. Clearly, their team was well aware of this and walked with a bit of a bounce in their step before the game started.

For this first contest our coach had the game plan totally down. He organized a mixture of offensive plays that isolated their team's weaknesses. He was also more affirming in his coaching with the players. It was a good game. The opposing team fought back several times, but in the end our team prevailed. Christopher didn't play the entire game, but he finished with nine points, five rebounds, and four assists. That was pretty good for the first night out under game conditions. DS later gave me a note saying that Christopher had played a solid game. I knew then that he was looking beyond the past issues and was attempting to move forward.

It was definitely a new and more serious basketball year. Beginning in seventh grade, we had entered phase two of the parochial school handbook, which stated only the best players would play. The fifth- and sixth-grade rules, where everyone played for skill development, were no longer in effect. I looked down at the bench during a game, and it appeared to me that the innocence was gone. Our team was playing for keeps. Christopher was going to play as many minutes as it took to win the game. Sadly, Christopher's buddies were locked onto the pine with very little chance to play until the game had more or less been decided. It was difficult to watch, but I believed it did give the boys an early look at competitive life. Fifth- and sixth-grade basketball had been their time. The boys knew that continuing on in seventh grade bound them to a whole new set of expectations.

As always, Christopher had a knack for finding neutral ground, which gave Jen and me some solace about the limited playing time of the "have-nots." Christopher explained to the two of us that his goal was to play each game extremely hard with the hope of raising his team's score by twenty or thirty points. This way his pals would be able to play, and if they were lucky, they might even be able to play as early as the third quarter. I wondered if this altruistic tendency Christopher displayed was some innate part of his personality. Perhaps, though, it was more of a progression of painful interpersonal relationships where he had been dissed and thus knew he never wanted to see others affected that way.

As the season unfolded, Christopher's plan appeared to be working. The team jumped to a 5–0 start with an average twenty-point margin of victory. In fact, Christopher's plan had worked so well early on in the season that his pals were playing as much as he was. It seemed that everyone was getting to play again after all! And there was Christopher right in the center of it all, giving all the unlikely participating players high fives as they came out of the games after having their time on the court.

The Thanksgiving holiday came quickly, and our team had elevated its record to 7–0. Our family spent most of the holiday break watching our local parochial high school team play in its turkey tournament. It was interesting to watch, since Christopher really thought highly of the school's coach. A funny voice told me that Christopher and that coach were going to get to know each other really well in the future.

Christopher had his first unofficial visit to a Division I college basketball game during the Sunday of Thanksgiving break. When we arrived at the will-call booth to retrieve our game tickets, I wondered if Christopher knew what to expect. It was a big, crowded place with lots of action everywhere, but as we walked around the arena, Christopher, being his youthful self, seemed most interested in watching people go by. We found our courtside seats, and it was clear just from the atmosphere of the arena that this was going to be a good time. Jen and I observed Christopher watching all the well-developed athletes travel up and down the floor, and it was difficult for us to believe that our son would be filling out college applications in just five short years.

As we sat there with Christopher, who continued watching the game with a child-like innocence, we noticed the jumbo screen hanging from the ceiling at midcourt. The camera crew chose people from the audience to feature on the big screen. It may sound crazy, but Christopher had learned to cope with his hearing loss by developing an acute sense of sight. As he watched the big screen focus on a couple at the game, he leaned over to me and said, "That was cute." Then he began scanning the arena crowd. A moment later, Christopher very casually said to me, "Do you see them over there?"

I looked out at about five thousand people at one end of the arena. "I can't find them," I said.

Christopher pointed his finger and said, "They are right over there by the band."

This took me to a whole new level of *Where's Waldo*. Christopher and I continued to converse, and I realized once again that he definitely viewed the world differently than I did. Testing my theory, I nudged Jen, pointed to the screen, and said, "Can you find the couple on the screen over there by the band?"

She looked at me and said, "What? No way! Where do you see them?"

I thought to myself, everyone has their own gift. In Christopher's case, his vision compensated for his lack of hearing.

We enjoyed the game immensely, and afterward, Christopher was invited to shoot baskets on the floor. What fun for him in that huge arena! As I watched him be a kid on that big floor, I wondered where we were headed. Would Christopher play basketball in college? I knew the odds of that happening were thousands to one. It's an unfortunate numbers game with many thousands of high school players all looking to land those four or five roster spots on teams at the D1 level. Sadly, too, these pipe dreams for other young people could be as high as thirty thousand to one. I quickly snapped myself out of those thoughts. For now Christopher just needed to concentrate on completing the seventh grade and making the honor roll.

———▼———

I think young women of a certain class would have called it a debutante party, but in Christopher's case it was *ephphatha*, with his new unknown path just starting to "be opened." When we returned from our college visit, Christopher had a series of conference tournament games. The two of us once again found ourselves in a small farm town. The school's gym was so tiny that you would miss it if you weren't careful, which was exactly what I almost did. Christopher and I arrived early to the game and unknowingly parked right in front of the gym facility. I stepped out of our car and humbly asked a man in a food delivery truck where the gym was. He pointed about twenty feet away and said, "Right there." A little embarrassed, I thanked him for his time.

The gym itself was a cracker box, but the tournament got off to a good start. Our team won its first two games and as I watched those first two tournament victories knowing we had just come back from a college visit, I could see that ephphatha was very real in Christopher's life. Christopher was a key player in his team's ability to secure a spot in the finals.

For the championship game, our school was matched up against another parochial school. Sitting in the stands, Jen and I met a couple of parents from the competing school. As the game went on it became apparent that their team had two very strong players and their son was one of them. Christopher seemed to be a little more focused on his game, and I thought it was because hardware was on the line again. Our coach could see we had a size advantage, so he wanted more rebounds from Christopher.

There was a battle of wills among the boys right from the start. The game continued back and forth with lead changes, but in the end Christopher became more assertive and finalized the game with a double-double in rebounds and points. The parents from the opposing team were so congenial and felt that Christopher was a "special player." Christopher's coach also recognized him for his significant contributions to the tournament games, and he asked him to present the team trophy to the school when they returned. I congratulated Christopher and noticed how tightly he grasped the championship trophy. He had brought his A game to the tournament, but he also understood that it had taken an entire team to win that trophy.

In basketball, there is always a better player out there. Sometimes those players could be closer to one's own neighborhood than one might think. As a teenager I had walked with more than a small bounce in my step after I was named to the high school all-tournament team at a prominent holiday hoops game in the Chicago area. My wise dad, however, could always name another kid who had been given similar tournament recognition. I once looked up a kid's name that my dad had mentioned. I thought there was no way the boy could have beaten my record scoring twenty-six points in a championship tournament game. In fact, the kid had scored thirty-eight points, and this was before three-pointers! Thirty-plus years later, I watched my own son experience the importance of humbleness. Christopher played his next game against a small 1A Division school in our state. He scored twenty-two points and grabbed eleven rebounds for a terrific game, but another superstar on the court scored an effortless thirty-one points. It's funny to see life experiences repeated throughout the generations.

With the basketball season well under way, Christopher showed how good he had become at making new friends. A prime example came one night at a basketball outing in our hometown. Another Christian school was ranked second and was headed to the regional tournament for state championship play. Christopher's team was ranked number one, and the final game had both teams desiring victory. Christopher knew his team needed to band together in order to have a good run at the championship. He cashed in six assists that night while playing only a little more than half of the game. Afterward, fans from both sides could not stop talking about his passing.

After the game, he and I walked to the concession stand. When we entered the food and drink room, the opposing team's parents told Christopher that he had played excellent team ball against their squad.

"You did great out there," one of the parents said to Christopher. "You really know how to find the open guy."

Christopher, always the diplomat, said, "Thanks. It wasn't easy. Your whole team played hard."

Some of the opposing players also congratulated Christopher, then they offered him some of their pizza. I left him there to enjoy the company of his new buddies. I believed this was Christopher's way of reaching out and retaining as many new friends as possible.

Toward the end of the evening, I looked over and saw him still sitting with about eight boys from the other team. That team had just lost to Christopher's team by twenty points, and it did not matter to any of those boys. They could still hang out with each other even though things may not have gone their way out on the court.

For Christopher, these types of interaction were often limited to the sporting venue. He had learned this all too well over the seasons. I know he wondered why he hadn't been invited to as many sleepovers or birthday parties as the other team members. He hadn't quite figured out that it was because he was different. Sadly, some of the twelve- and thirteen-year-old boys and their parents didn't open up and spend the extra time necessary to accommodate Christopher. The exceptions to this rule were people who had experience with disabled folks. Those families tended to feel more comfortable inviting Christopher over. One of Christopher's teammates lived with his disabled uncle, and he and Christopher became very good friends.

In January of 2009, the regional state tournament began and the seventh-grade version of March Madness—actually more of a February Frenzy—was on! In our state, which is four hundred miles long and nearly one hundred and fifty miles wide, it was the pinnacle of the basketball season for all the junior high school teams throughout the vast state.

For his part, Christopher had a less than awesome start to the tournament. In game one, he was in foul trouble for only the second time in twenty-two games that year. He quickly fouled two times during the beginning of the game, and the coach benched him for the remainder of the first half. Coaching etiquette dictated that the coach would not want to risk Christopher getting a third foul, which would put him in foul trouble during the second half of the game as well. Coaching etiquette aside, Christopher's coach put him back into the game with just sixteen seconds left in the first half. What do you think happened? He fouled someone. The mistake landed Christopher back on the bench for a good part of the second half of the game. Afterward, Christopher asked me why his coach had done that. In my best Christian persona, I responded, "Son, you have to forgive him. He is only human."

As the state tournament progressed, I realized that sometimes in life the stars align themselves in a way that was meant to be. Such was the case that cold January in our hometown. Our team had advanced to the regional tournament finals, and it would be a battle of two prominent parochial schools. Our team was matched up against our nemesis from across town. This opposing school's drubbings went back to when our daughter had played basketball. Against Rachel's squad, the school's team had been relentless with their pressure defense and combined scoring at will. I remembered one year when my daughter's team had scored one—yes, *one*—point in the entire game against the school.

This year, however, Christopher's team came into the game with an 18–5 record, and most of his team's losses had been at the hands of much larger schools than his.

The game began with a buzz due to the opposing school supplying a referee from another one of its sports teams to officiate the game. So it seemed already that things might be stacked against us. Questionable officiating or not, Christopher's squad struggled throughout the game. Even though we were ranked as the number one team in the area, it surely did not show so far. At halftime, our team had barely inched ahead.

The second half didn't start out much better. The opposing players were hitting almost all of their shots while our team was not playing up to its standards. I looked up at the clock. We were down by five with less than two minutes to go in the game. One of our players took the ball to the hoop and had a potential three-point play. Unfortunately, he missed the free throw. But our luck appeared to be changing. The opposing team turned the ball over again, and Christopher made a basket. We were now down by one. Then a foul in the other team's favor put their best player on the line. The tension was palpable. Stunning everyone in the gymnasium, the player missed both of his free throws. The stage was set then as one of our players dribbled the ball up the sideline. In those remaining seconds, Christopher moved out of his position and established himself in a new spot three feet in front of the basket. Our player couldn't help but get him the ball.

Christopher had his own method to bypass some of the guards' tunnel vision. He would scream out, "Ball!" I sat next to a college coaching buddy of mine as we watched Christopher's coach almost simultaneously yell back, "GIVE IT TO HIM!" The ball immediately landed in Christopher's hands. He powered it to the basket and was fouled. At the line, Christopher hit one free throw and rimmed the next, tying the game. The opposing team quickly and nervously tossed the ball out of bounds. I looked up and saw fifteen seconds on the clock.

I guess the old saying "If it ain't broke, don't fix it" applied at this point. Just as quickly as one could look, that ball went back to Christopher. He was fouled again. While the other team's fans screamed, Christopher went one for two again, and our team was up by one. The opposition passed the ball quickly up the floor but missed a shot with three seconds left. Christopher grabbed the rebound and was fouled. He calmly moved to the free-throw line and sank two free throws in a row while the crowd yelled wildly. I wondered how much the Deaf kid had heard. The final score was 33–30. Once again, Christopher's coach asked him to present the trophy to the school on Monday.

———▾———

The following week, we drove an hour and a half south to a small community for sectional play. The winner would go to the elite eight state tournament. An opposing team with a 17–1 record awaited us. The pesky guards on this team had probably played together since first grade, and they had us down by about fifteen points at the half. During the intermission, our crowd seemed to be thinking, *Oh well, good season.* I couldn't really blame them. A team that was that far down at the half would have a difficult hill to climb. However, as the second half began, it seemed like divine intervention was on our side. That, or perhaps Christopher was possessed. He took over that game himself, scoring eight points in the final quarter. The win made us sectional champs, and we were off to the state finals.

The following Saturday, our team went up against the sectional winner from the west-central part of the state. We were from the east-central portion of the state. It was hard for us to not feel like we were in the movie *Hoosiers*. Our sectional opponent had played at the state tournament in recent years, so they understood the feel of championship play. Our school, on the other hand, hadn't played in a state tournament since 1943, and even then, it had been for a fourth-place finish.

The state tournament atmosphere was amazing. When our boys arrived, they were immediately escorted into the gym for a tour and then had their pictures taken in a special area. Yes, welcome to the big time, where ticket prices were seven dollars and glossy state championship programs cost five dollars. The gym was located just outside the state capital, and it was many times bigger than any other place our team had ever played. There was a college-style scoreboard and a public announcer who sounded so cool that we were all pinching ourselves while waiting for the game to begin.

Christopher would test that public announcer right from the start with the introduction of the team's players. We listened as his long name boomed over the gym's system so all could hear. It came again on the first basket, CHRISTOPHER CAULFIELD. And again on each of our team's second and third baskets, CHRISTOPHER CAULFIELD. Christopher had been in a zone from opening tipoff, and his team carried home a victory and a date with the final four.

How amazing was that? There were just four teams left from our big state that covered fifty-seven thousand square miles: one team from the north, one from the south, and two teams right from the middle of the state. Our boys were excited to play—maybe too excited. Their final four opponent was more than they could handle, and our team was off to play in the third-place game. But once again, our team was outscored by a very good team. When it was all over, we had secured the fourth-place trophy for our school. Although our team's goals might have been lofty, our boys would always remember that they had finished as high as any other team in their school's hundred-plus-year history.

Basketball season came to a close. While our family was very grateful for an outstanding year, it was now time for us to look toward spring. Another growth check on Christopher revealed that he had already grown another half inch in March, putting him well over the six-foot mark. He was asked to participate on the school track team, but he elected not to join. He had seriously considered participating in cross-country, but I thought this had more to do with the fact that the sport was coed, with lots of young women competing in the team's dual meets.

Christopher continued to excel academically, becoming a fixture on the honor roll. Socially, not much had changed, however. I wished that his teammates would stay in touch with him even though the season was over. Unfortunately, he was once again left out of the social circles. It was my hope that, as his friends matured, they would become more empathic toward Christopher's needs.

Christopher opted to place his efforts elsewhere. One April day he said to me, "Dad, do you think lifting a lot of weights on the off-season is bad?" I turned to an old acquaintance, the strength and conditioning coach at the Big Ten university in our town, to answer that question. "It is okay in moderation" was the verdict. Given the overall questionable research on weightlifting's effects on a person's growth at the time, Jen and I encouraged Christopher to work out with lower weights and higher repetitions. Even with the lower weights, Christopher was able to increase both his muscle mass and his weight, which neared a whopping one hundred and forty pounds at age thirteen. We observed changes in both his physique and our grocery bill!

Spring marched on, and our family faced an important basketball decision. Should Christopher travel with an AAU team throughout the Midwest, or should he play closer to home? Christopher made his case: "You know, Dad, I have been able to play against a lot of great players from our state. I wonder what it would be like to play really good ones from other states?"

With that, I knew that if Christopher had his druthers, he would elect to travel more. The dilemma was that extensive travel meant a bit less participation in local basketball summer camps. Those camps could lead to more and different opportunities. But when a prominent Midwest AAU coach called us and waived Christopher's tryout option, the deal was sealed. Elite AAU basketball, here we come!

———◦———

Also that spring, Christopher was honored with a request to speak to a group of donors at our local hospital. His speech would assist the hospital in its multimillion-dollar campaign to build a new center and school for the Deaf. Christopher had been the very first student at the original school in 1997, when he was a little over a year old. Now he stood in front of the donors as a thirteen-year-old young man.

Christopher's speech was flawless. He marveled the audience right from the start by describing his own personal journey throughout the last decade. His message was loud and clear: Excellence comes from hard work and a great family support system.

At the end of the speech, someone in the audience asked Christopher what one of his biggest accomplishments was. After a five-second pause, Christopher said, "Well, before I die (pause), I want to look back and say that through all of my hard work, I was able to talk pretty well and be like everybody else.

"You see, when I was little, I used to watch all of these kids my age come into McDonald's and order their food from the counter all by themselves. I could never do that. Now I, too, walk up to the counter, reach into my pocket to get the money out, and then order my four hamburgers, an order of fries, and some water because I've got to watch my weight." When Christopher was finished, there wasn't a dry eye in the house.

CHAPTER 6

ELITE AAU BALL AND BASKETBALL CAMPS

————▼————

If there ever was a time for Christopher to find out if he really enjoyed playing basketball, it was during the summer of 2009. In addition to the AAU team he had agreed to join, he had ten basketball camps on his radar during those lazy days of summer. The first camp was right in our hometown at a school with a strong basketball reputation. The previous year, Christopher had earned hardware as one of the camp's top players. This year, it quickly became apparent that the one-on-one champ would be the player who earned the lone trophy.

Christopher started the one-on-one play facing a boy who reminded many of Biff, the bully from the movie *Back to the Future*. It wasn't Christopher's first encounter with Biff. Not too long before, he had witnessed Biff taking the tennis balls off of the chair legs at school and throwing them at the backs of his classmates. On that occasion, a tennis ball hit Christopher in the back of the head and knocked his implant off. Not surprisingly, there hadn't been one ounce of regret from Biff. On the court, Christopher was able to outlast Biff in what he thought was the last time he would have to play him in the one-on-one tournament.

Unfortunately, Christopher soon learned that these tough one-on-one games were nothing more than warm-up exercises. As the competition escalated, Christopher advanced nicely over five other young men. The final matchup pitted Christopher against Biff.

The championship was a game of finesse versus brawn. The key play of the game occurred near the end of the contest, when Christopher challenged Biff's jump shot. The result was an air ball. Once Christopher saw the ball fall short of the hoop, he only ran half speed, thinking it didn't matter since Biff couldn't rebound the ball. It would be an illegal pass to himself. But Biff didn't see it that way. He grabbed the ball and laid it in the hoop for the winning shot. The ref's whistle was silent and the score counted. The campers roared their disapproval but it didn't change the outcome. Christopher had lost.

Afterward, I informed Christopher that the referee had made a judgment call in determining whether or not Biff's shot had been legitimate. Since in the referee's judgment it was a sincere effort to score, the result was a free ball for anyone to grab—including Biff. The moral of the story for Christopher was to finish every play!

————▼————

AAU basketball. Some say it is responsible for the eroding of high school basketball. I'm not sure that is the case, since if you go into most communities you will find that attendance at high school games is rolling along nicely. There is no debate, however, that elite AAU ball is where a player will find out if he has the right stuff to play at the next level. As the major elite-level tournaments are set up in regions of the country, the players on these teams have a plan. They are not playing to get in shape or for recreational purposes. They are continually slicing up the pie of excellent players and teams until there is only one group left. And this will go on annually over the number of years the young player competes in AAU. In the end, after years of ongoing AAU ball throughout high school, around fifty players are left standing, nationally. For the most serious AAU players, that is the top of the mountain. The attention is endless for this group, with hundreds of D1 college basketball scholarship offers and the biggest recognition they will receive in their basketball career to date: All-American.

Before Christopher joined his AAU team, he met with the coach. He liked that the coach was not only a former assistant for a Division I program but was also the captain and point guard of his collegiate team. Christopher was given the signs for all the basketball plays as early as the second practice. Our family once again thanked God for an accommodating coach who effectively worked with Christopher's disability.

I was amazed at how much more competitive AAU was that year. Christopher played five or six games across Saturday and Sunday during an average AAU travel ball weekend. I liked to think that Christopher was a good-sized forward or center as an eighth grader, but when I attended a competitive AAU weekend, I discovered there were plenty of talented, good-sized athletes in these same positions.

Some of these players came from the southern part of our state, while others came from the western area. What really mattered, though, was that they had all previously played on their school's state championship, elite eight–level team while just in seventh grade. Christopher and I also noted that two of the top players had led their teams to undefeated regular seasons. One of the centers was six feet one inch, while the other was six-foot-three. Those impressive heights made Christopher's height appear almost average.

So there we were, joining another new group. But somehow this was very different from earlier teams and in a way that caused me to think Christopher was without a doubt going to meet his match. After just a year or two on an AAU team, many of these players would try out for the varsity team as freshmen at their high school. As I watched some of the more phenomenal players dunking before they had even started eighth grade, I knew this was where players found out if they could compete at the next level.

Christopher's weekends that summer were all AAU ball, and his weekdays were filled with basketball camps. One busy camp day schedule included attending a public high school camp from 8:00 to 10:00 a.m., another high school camp from 10:30 a.m. to 12:30 p.m., a lunch break with rest, and then a final afternoon camp at a rural school from 3:00 to 4:30 p.m. In addition, Christopher had AAU ball practice two evenings a week. It was so busy some weeks, we were relieved when the last camp concluded. On the final day, Christopher finished second in shooting to the son of a Big Ten player, and he won runner-up to a high school player at another camp. While he was extremely disappointed to come in second, I was very proud of him. What's more, the coaches looked at Christopher and saw a six-foot-tall kid who brought kind of a European finesse to his game.

I, on the other hand, was experiencing mixed emotions about all that we were just starting to encounter. It seemed like we had suddenly entered an "arms race." If you wanted to keep up with the best players, then you simply had to be invited to try out for the elite AAU teams. If you were invited—and Christopher was—then what do you do? Well, like Christopher, you go to the tryout and hope you do your best that day. When Christopher made the team, he never really pondered whether or not to play. He chose to play and Jen and I supported him. For camps it was entirely different. With camps it was more of a quest to be in a hoops environment on an ongoing basis. A basketball camp allowed players to get tons of exposure on a daily basis to fundamentals, strategy, guest speakers, and even some workshops on the critical importance of studies. With all that Christopher was doing, the whole family was immersed in the world of basketball.

One of the early camps Christopher attended was at a Big Ten school. Most people would probably assume that a basketball camp at a Big Ten school would bring in some really great talent. While it was fair to say that the talent was really good, it was not excellent. The problem was that this type of camp was expensive. The kids who came from lower-income families usually found that a sponsored AAU team was a better fit for them. The games at this camp, however, proved to still be competitive, so I felt good about Christopher attending.

I admired Christopher's competitive instincts as I observed some of his games, but I also noted that he would have some tough lessons to learn down the road as well. He was involved in one game that was nip and tuck down to the final seconds. While his team barely stayed ahead, the other team fouled in an attempt to get the ball back. This brought one of Christopher's fellow players, who enjoyed scoring, to the line for a one-and-one. If he made the first shot, he'd earn a second one. Unfortunately, he missed. The other squad then took the ball for a potential win. They turned the ball over and fouled again, and our same guy stepped up to the line. Against the odds, he missed his shot again. The opposing coach quickly called a timeout.

In the huddle, Christopher went right up to his dejected teammate and said, "You have to make those free throws." With the timeout concluded, the opposing team missed a heave and our team won the game.

Afterward, the coach gave Christopher a well-deserved private talk about how to talk to his teammates. What the coach didn't know was that the line "You have to make those free throws" went a little deeper for Christopher. At a past AAU game, one of the coaches had told another player to relay that exact same command to Christopher. Which coach had wanted that? Me. We were in a tight game, and Christopher had initiated a new shot that summer. The result was that he went two for twelve from the line in one of our games. In an act of frustration, I called a timeout, looked directly at one of Christopher's teammates, and asked him for his thoughts. One of our best players looked Christopher in the eye and said, "You gotta make those free throws."

The situation was not embarrassing, since we had a tight team. The situation was different on a summer camp team where the players were only together for a few days. Christopher had obviously remembered this past calling-out, and he repeated it to his fellow camper as a teachable moment in his mind. Unfortunately, Christopher hadn't yet formed enough of a relationship with this camp player to make such a comment, and the coach now thought Christopher had a questionable attitude. His teammate too probably thought Christopher was just plain full of himself. It was a lesson that Christopher would not soon forget.

⎯⎯⎯▾⎯⎯⎯

AAU ball took Christopher and me to a tournament in Indiana later that month. As always, we encountered a serious blend of basketball there. Unlike many states, Indiana had been dramatically divided by its college basketball fan base. South of Indianapolis was Hoosier land, north was Notre Dame, and the central section of the state was Purdue and Butler territory. Basketball in Indiana was ginormous at the high school level as well, with the top four gyms in the state having capacity to hold eight thousand–plus fans. Indiana was simply obsessed with basketball. On this particular occasion, we were at Purdue University, but teams came from all over the state and you could feel the proud history of Indiana basketball.

Overall, our team was playing pretty well in the tournament. Christopher was averaging thirteen points, six rebounds, and three assists per game. His coach was very happy with his play. He had been very clear with his assistant coach that when the game was on the line, they needed to draw the play up for Christopher to make the difference. In our final game, though, tension began to surface. The players had started to get edgy near the end of the game, as most of the boys were being outplayed. Those watching could feel this one slipping away. Out on the court, Christopher called one of the other players out about what he deemed to be selfish play. A good coach will in these situations look for the players to rally themselves on the court with group huddles during stoppages in play. Our coach was great at this and he let them try to figure it out themselves before having to call a timeout. Unfortunately, things only got worse on the court, so the timeout was eventually called. As I watched the team gathering on the sideline, I noticed that the players wouldn't budge when Christopher attempted to get a chair near the coach. Christopher lost his cool and yelled for them to move. Once I realized what was happening, I immediately asked the coach to take Christopher out of the game, which he did.

Later, I thanked the coach for listening to me. The drama of it all! I thought there was most likely a pretty simple explanation for what had happened on the bench. The players on the team stuck together in pairs, and Christopher's hearing and speaking disability made him the odd man out. While I knew that none of the boys were necessarily bad kids, I realized that they would rather look out for their own buddies than for the kid who couldn't hear what they were saying most of the time when they were in the loud gym. That game allowed me to see the struggle Christopher went through in a moment of frustration and even desperation as he tried to place his chair close enough to the coach to be able to hear.

———▼———

Our next stop was at another Big Ten camp with more than three hundred attendees. The participants ranged in age from seven to seventeen years old. I had heard that this camp was very strong, so I signed Christopher up for a two-week session. The camp, like most others, began with the team selection. To my surprise, Christopher was the second tallest boy in the thirteen-year-old group during his first week. I suspected that this wouldn't have been the case last summer when he had been twelve years old, but regardless, it was interesting to see his height trajectory was still pretty much in line with all his medical growth charts. There were about sixty-five boys in his thirteen-year-old class, and I figured that Christopher was sitting in the top three percent in height.

I had to hand it to the head Big Ten coach hosting the camp. He was a decent guy who was congenial, positive, and available for both the players and the parents. It was a welcome change from some of the past camps where the head coaches greeted the parents and then disappeared for the remainder of the week.

The camp went along nicely for Christopher. His team was strong and made it to the final four. They were eventually outscored by the future team camp champion, but Christopher learned a valuable lesson. In order for a player to be considered the top camper, he had to first win the team competition. It played out exactly that way when a six-foot-tall center played well in the championship game and then deservedly won the Camper of the Week award. I was thankful that Christopher had vicariously experienced this, so he would understand what it might take to win that award in the upcoming week's camp.

After a few days off, Christopher returned to the Big Ten camp for another three and a half days. By now, Christopher was definitely getting the hang of this camp thing. He began the camp by winning a shooting contest. By the time the week was almost over, he had competed in the three-on-three championship as well. Christopher's team continued to excel. They could finally celebrate having the best camp record for five-on-five competition.

However, something very unusual happened on the last day. In a camp with more than three hundred boys, one teammate was traded for another. Christopher's coach removed him from the top team and traded him to a team that had not won a single game. At the same time, a non-impact player was transferred to the top team. My initial thought was probably similar to Christopher's: how could the coach move him off of his team on championship game day? I also thought that Christopher's opportunity to win the Camper of the Week award was looking slim. Even more disconcerting was that Christopher was moved just after he had gotten to know his nine other teammates. So much for a coach understanding the time it takes a Deaf kid to acclimate to his new situation.

Nevertheless, Christopher quickly recovered. He put up six points in each of his quarters, along with three, fun-to-watch assists in his new team's first and only win. Our goal going in had been for Christopher to receive the Camper of the Week award. The trade made that goal virtually impossible. I considered why the coach would have made such an unprecedented move. My conclusion was that the coaches did not want to send a team home with no wins, as that would not be a positive experience for those players. I suppose we should have been flattered in a way that they clearly knew if there was one young man at the camp to earn that win for a lone disenfranchised team, it was Christopher. Christopher also learned an important skill: how to go into an unpleasant situation and still get through it successfully. In the end, I was very proud to see him step up in such an altruistic role.

After the camp, I felt kind of silly for being so obsessed with winning the Camper of the Week award. While he didn't capture that one, he came home with four other awards. Christopher and I thanked all of the coaches for their efforts and in our hearts knew that an unanticipated accomplishment had come our way that week.

It was now nearing the end of July, and we were headed to a Five Star, Division I camp in Indiana. I've always wondered where the name Hoosiers originated. The best explanation I heard came from one of my colleagues, who had been born and raised in Indiana. As he explained it, the people in Indiana really trusted each other in their neighborhoods. It was not uncommon for many of the people in the state to leave their doors unlocked. Usually when a visitor knocked on a house door, the person inside would say, "Who's there?" If you roughly shorten that response, you get *Hoosier*. To put it simply, the people of Indiana were salt of the earth types who enjoyed bonding together as Hoosiers!

I wished for Christopher to have a welcome arrival at his Five Star camp. Five Star was huge. Christopher did not know it but many high school basketball All-Americans at one point in their young basketball careers played there. The first young man we saw warming up in the gym stood six feet two inches tall, and I was later informed that this player had already verbally committed to Michigan State. Luckily for the campers, he was just shooting around in the gym in Fort Wayne by coincidence as the thirteen- and fourteen-year-old Five Star folks were checking in.

Five Star was a three-day experience. Just like all the previous camps, Christopher and I commuted there, but in this case, our commute was to and from the hotel. This allowed Christopher to get a better night's sleep than he would have in the facility dorm. As always, we just couldn't take the chance that Christopher would safely escape should there be a fire, since he could not hear the alarm system. I knew I wouldn't be able to live with myself if he were to ever become trapped in a building.

A significant number of players were scoping out each other's abilities during day one of the camp. When Christopher returned to the hotel that evening, I asked how it had gone.

"It was all right," he said. "Kind of boring, though. Most of the other kids seem to think they're better than they are."

"Well, you might be interested to know I met with the camp coordinator. He's the one who used to coach college ball."

"You did? What did he say?"

"He said he already could see that you're a special player for your age."

"Really? Cool. But it seemed like most of the guys there today were just out for themselves."

I said, "That's not so surprising, is it? These guys know that Five Star is not for teenagers who are less than serious about basketball." Christopher nodded his head in agreement. Then I said, "They are playing for keeps, Christopher. Many of these guys want to play in college and most of them probably will compete for a varsity spot as freshmen in high school."

We kind of stared at each other after that, and I wondered if Christopher wouldn't have had a better summer riding his bike around the neighborhood and swimming at the pool.

On day two, Christopher's coaches began to take even more notice of him. In the afternoon, they worked with Christopher and a few other players on signaling plays. On day three, I sensed that Christopher was on the verge of something really big as he took everything he had learned over the previous two days and put it all into action. He scored thirteen points, six rebounds, and four assists in the final scrimmage, and his team was crowned the camp champions. He also landed the top award at Five Star for fifteen-year-olds in the sharp shooting competition even though he was just thirteen years old. We sure felt welcome in the Hoosier state!

In the Midwest where our family lived, it wasn't just Big Ten country. It was also home to a few Missouri Valley schools, and that's where we were headed next. The head basketball coach of the camp's host school was popularly known to emphasize education first to his athletes. Heck, he was an Academic All-American himself, so he definitely brought that cerebral mentality to his team. Christopher recognized some familiar faces from grade school basketball also participating in the camp.

Two twin boys were six feet two inches tall and had already commanded the majority of the coaches' attention. They were quite the sight, actually, being so much bigger, stronger, and faster than all the other boys at the camp.

Although Christopher's team didn't finish on top during the week of camp, I was delighted when the school's director of basketball operations called to inform me that Christopher had once again caught the coaches' eyes. The camp director extended an invitation for Christopher to attend a 2009 game of his choice at the university.

While Christopher was wrapping up his week of camp, a recruit who was six feet eight inches tall announced that he had chosen another school over the camp's host institution. This recruit was an all-state forward, and I envisioned Christopher developing into a similar player one day if his growth continued its steady pattern. Interestingly, the recruit's dad was also at this camp as a counselor. Would this turn into a touchy situation, since his son had just orally committed to a rival school in the same conference? I later had the opportunity to talk with the recruit's dad and was thankful to hear that things between himself and the school remained amicable. In his mind the selection of school for his son came down to "fit." You could tell his dad was a humble man and thus his son moving in a different direction was not going to be a rift at all. His dad also had many positive things to say about Christopher's potential as a basketball player. "Christopher's shooting ability is remarkable, as is his ability to handle the ball. Especially for a big kid," he said. I could tell he was reminded of how his son had played just a few years prior. It was great to talk with him, as he struck me as a guy who wasn't too caught up in all the stress of college selection based on basketball. The director of basketball operations walked us all out as the camp concluded, and I was once again reminded to simply enjoy the recruitment process without letting myself or our thirteen-year-old get too caught up in things.

Christopher and Brian Cook

With summer quickly winding down, Christopher and I had just two camps remaining. One of these camps, Hoop Mountain, was new to us. The camp's descriptive literature basically read that if a player was not extremely serious about basketball, he shouldn't even bother signing up for the all-star camp. The other camp, Brian Cook, was an annual stop for us. In fact, Christopher was honored to be on a first-name basis with Brian, who was a star player for the Los Angeles Lakers at the time. In reality, though, Christopher was more of a Larry Bird "wanna-be." He wore a No.

33 jersey on his AAU team, and more than a few Indiana referees had remarked that Christopher's pure form in the shot pocket closely resembled Bird's. I had to admit that six-foot-tall Christopher, with his blond wavy hair, fair skin, and lanky torso, also resembled Larry Bird. Further, like Bird, Christopher was a basketball gym rat who was always interested in finding a game to participate in. As an academic professional, I was able to get him guest passes to our Big Ten university's recreation center. It was common on a busy day for ten basketball games to be going on there at once. Luckily for us, the courts weren't quite as full in the summer, and Christopher was still able to get in plenty of practice. The rec center's court structure was a pecking order of who had game, with the winner staying on court. In other words, it was survival of the best ballers.

On our first trip to the rec center, we noticed three or four groups of young men aged seventeen to twenty-five playing on the courts. The group on the lowest rung of the ladder was composed of the academic types who enjoyed running up and down the court while being generally indifferent about winning or losing. Sophomores and juniors, who had most likely played some form of organized ball before college, made up the second group. Their obvious goal was to play on the top court with the best players. Who were the best players? They were the group of guys who had played ball in high school and college. On occasion, Christopher and I had also observed the university's football players playing, but the real sight to see was when the school's own basketball players showed up to take the court. For the most part, Christopher played very well on the high school–level court. There were, however, a couple of times when I watched him climb his way to top-court play. He was indeed a gym rat who lived and breathed basketball.

Christopher and I arrived at a small, private college in the Midwest for his second to last camp that summer. When he checked in on the first day, he was given a reversible jersey with the number 222. We knew then that this would be a well-attended, competitive camp. Even the camp's coaches represented a wide variety of areas in the state.

The camp began with free shooting in the different gyms. As we strolled by one gym, the competition seemed right up Christopher's alley, but another gym appeared to have more advanced players. My mind raced ahead. I thought, "Those guys are way too mature for Christopher; he's only entering the eighth grade." It turned out that the advanced players were the high school guys. Whew! Once we found his age group, I saw that thirteen-year-old Christopher was once again one of the taller boys on the court.

There was only one boy taller than Christopher, and he was a six-foot three-inch-tall seventh grader. Judging by the previous camps, I knew that Christopher would inevitably be matched up against this big player. The days were heavy at this camp. Optional fundamental work began at 7:30 a.m., and there were only two breaks: lunch and dinner. Christopher and I typically headed home around 9:30 p.m. each night. Overall, it was two and a half days of hard work, but the camp ultimately played out well for Christopher. His team made it to the championship and outlasted the competing team by two points.

The real highlight of the camp experience, however, had been Christopher's participation in a computerized shooting system. The system had a very sophisticated camera that took hundreds of pictures in about five seconds and was able to measure the arc of a fifteen-foot jump shot. The computer would then compare a player's arc to other players from the grade school level up to the professional ranks. Research from hundreds of NBA players indicated that forty-three degrees was the optimal arc for a fifteen-foot jump shot. Further, the best pros could consistently shoot from fifteen feet away with only a one- or two-degree variance in arc. Chris Mullin, who played for St. John's in college and the Indiana Pacers in the pros, was the top player ever to be recorded on the computer system.

As I stood talking to a coach in the gym, the person operating the shooting system wanted to meet with me. He held the results and pictures of Christopher's arc in his hands. He explained in excitement, "Christopher scored at Expert III!" This placed Christopher in a category well beyond his age. It further validated my belief that his disability had led to his greater visual discrimination. Christopher's shooting results placed his arc between forty-one and forty-four degrees, which was essentially the arc of an NBA rookie. According to the camp operator, only one college camp counselor had matched Christopher's shooting score on the system that week.

Christopher's last camp before school started was with Brian Cook. I remembered the first camp that Brian had put together with a couple of his college buddies. Those buddies were now either coaching or playing in the NBA as well. The camp was held at one of our local Christian schools, and what a great camp it was. In those days, all of the players from Brian's past teams attended his camps. They simply enjoyed giving back to the community and spending their day with young people. These players not only taught the campers basketball skills, but they also extensively incorporated life skills and interpersonal effectiveness into their camp instruction. I especially appreciated how they broke down these interpersonal skills into smaller lessons and later turned them into effective role plays with the camp players.

Christopher's coach for the week was a former Big Ten basketball player himself. Since Christopher was over six feet tall now, his new coach thought he should be playing with the sophomore and junior kids. When I questioned his coach about this, explaining that Christopher was only entering eighth grade, he said, "Oh, wow! I thought he was in high school. But no worries. I think he can definitely hang with the older guys." As the camp went on, it became clear that Christopher's play was above average as compared to the other fifteen- and sixteen-year-old boys there, which was fine by me.

After camp ended, some even better news came our way. Christopher was recognized in our city newspaper for having been the first student at the Carle School for the Deaf. A private donor had contributed a large amount of money to build a new eight-million-dollar school, and Christopher was honored to have a room in the new building named after him. The *News-Gazette* carried the story.

CHAPTER 7

———————▼———————

In August of 2009, Christopher celebrated his fourteenth birthday and our daughter, Rachel, celebrated her eighteenth. Rachel was studying journalism at the University of Illinois at Urbana-Champaign (UIUC). Hmmm… what a book she could have written, having grown up with her lone Deaf sibling! It must have crossed her mind as she watched Christopher struggling to make a go in life. Writing may have even been therapeutic for her given all the challenges she had observed while growing up. Our reality was that without Rachel and her ongoing support for her brother, Christopher would not be as accomplished as he was going into the eighth grade.

Our daughter participated in the convocation at the beginning of her time at UIUC. This event was something of a pep rally to get all the freshmen excited about college. It's a small world; the keynote speaker was an acquaintance of mine. As a Pulitzer Prize–winning journalist, he was no intellectual small fry. His address to the new students was stunning. He remarked that out of the thirty thousand to forty thousand students on campus, at least a thousand dealt with very serious disabilities. His point was that college could be an extremely lonely place for a person with a disability. I know our daughter must have reflected on this information as she remembered growing up with her own disabled brother. I could not help but ponder this myself, since my dad had also been disabled. I had witnessed him struggling in so many ways. My friend's message was simple. He encouraged his audience to take the extra step to reach out to the disabled because only God knew how lonely and withdrawn their lives could be.

As Rachel told us her impressions of the speech, I was astonished by her take on it. She said, "He is right, you know, that people many times don't know how they can reach out in support for those with disabilities." Her eyes then got very focused, almost like she was running a movie in her head of all the things she had done in her fourteen years with Christopher to help him. "I sometimes wonder what if it was me that was the Deaf one in our family," she said. "I know Christopher just being who he is would help me. But I also know from my experience something comes over you where you simply jump in and help as best as you can. And I have to tell you that I actually have gained so many things from going through our situation that clearly have helped me accomplish the things I have."

As a dad I reflected on her thoughts and knew immediately, with Rachel off at school, the world was going to be her oyster. She seemed to have no emotional scars left behind but rather the great feeling that she did her best for our family and her brother.

In the early fall of 2009, in addition to Rachel being gone, I noticed another void in our family life. I had experienced this feeling during the prior spring season, and

High school and college siblings

it all came together in my mind. It was a soccer void. This would be the first time in five years that Christopher wasn't playing soccer. I once heard that, come fall, football guys could smell the autumn air and instinctively be ready for the gridiron. Similarly, our family was used to attending soccer practices and games. A candid Christopher had indicated to us that he really just wanted to concentrate on one sport, hoops. While he didn't seem to regret not playing soccer that year, I wondered if he understood just how much his parents missed their weekly social interactions with the other soccer parents. Oh well, the life of parents meant going with the flow and continuing to nurture their young.

By that time, Christopher had been playing soccer largely for the cardiovascular workout. With all the intensity of AAU and the many camps he had participated in, he was as fit as could be going into the fall. But with basketball season still a number of weeks off, Christopher started looking for some sort of in-between maintenance program to keep him where he was physically. Jen and I thought a preseason conditioning program might be a reasonable substitute for soccer. Christopher agreed.

The fitness center in our town was promoting a preseason basketball training program, and it was to take place at an optimal time for our new schedule. We thought this program would also be good for Christopher's goals of enhancing his strength, agility, and quickness. Perhaps even more fun for Christopher would be the group he was to compete with. There was one high school senior, two juniors, a sophomore, and a freshman. Christopher being only in the eighth grade would feel as if he were playing with the big guys.

Christopher's true test came with a competition known as the pacer test. The pacer test is a twenty-yard interval evaluation where participants run on a series of tone signals. Now, Christopher's trainer was hearing impaired himself. Although not profoundly Deaf, he understood Christopher's needs perhaps more than any other coach. From day one I could see Christopher would receive any and all accommodations he needed to level the playing field. As the pacer test started, Christopher's trainer had that tone jacked so loud that there was no doubt Christopher would hear it.

The tricky part of this test was that the tones would sound in shorter time intervals as the run went on. The participants, upon hearing the tone, would attempt to traverse the twenty yards and cross the line at the other end, where they would prepare for the next tone. In the beginning the timing was such that the players could jog and sometimes wait at the end of the line until the next tone sounded, signaling them to go again. The tone came about once every seven seconds to start, but the intervals shortened incrementally by split seconds. After about thirty tone bursts, the freshmen and lone sophomore were finished. Next went the juniors and the senior. Christopher was left to run the race on his own. When finished, each player's performance was converted to a score. Christopher's score was an amazing ninety-two out of one hundred. That tied a school record set when Christopher's grade school physical education class had run the same drill.

——————▼——————

Some of the world's best scholars believe that the true measure of our society is determined by how we treat the needy and disenfranchised. For the previous four years, Jen and I had been actively questioning the leadership of Christopher's parochial school. The number of families leaving the school indicated to us there was a problem. The latest school issue was the concept of bullying, and we never thought it would affect Christopher as directly as it did that year.

I picked up Christopher from school every day. One afternoon, I noticed that he was running a little late to the car. As I waited, a parent came up to me in the parking lot and said, "You know we have a state tournament game for baseball today, right?"

I responded, "Yes, at 4:45 p.m." I then wished her luck.

She dismissed my response and stated, "The boys are saying that someone spilled ink in the classroom, so the teacher is keeping everyone in the room until the person who did it admits to it. The students are also saying that Christopher did it."

I wished that this parent had Christopher's best interest at heart while relaying this information to me, but unfortunately, her past behavior left me feeling skeptical. In my mind, her ulterior motive was that the boys had a baseball game to get to, and the prominent baseball players in the room had been delayed. I thanked Mrs. Anti-Altruism and headed up to Christopher's classroom.

When I arrived, Christopher was sitting alone on one side of the room with his head down and his face beet red. The students in the class had clearly separated themselves from him. As the teacher put it, they were trying to "throw Christopher under the bus." I informed the teacher of my intentions and then asked Christopher to step outside of the classroom to talk with me. The baseball moms were also standing outside of the classroom waiting for their children, and they looked to us for some sort of relief. It felt funny to me that Christopher's character was not known by these parents. I mean, had they really known Christopher it would have been obvious to them that if Christopher spilled the ink he would admit to it.

Out in the hall, I asked Christopher to tell me what was up. "The guys are just looking for someone to blame," he said. "They chose me because I'm not on the baseball team."

I went back into the classroom and told the teacher that Christopher had done nothing wrong, and we left. That was a very quiet ride home that day. I could tell that Christopher knew he was actively picked to take the blame. To him that meant he was not accepted. I thought it was sad but I knew that was how some kids could be. No matter how great a basketball player he was and how many trophies he presented to the school,

Christopher, it seemed, could not overcome being the scapegoat. Maybe since his teacher knew Christopher could not have done this, she was holding all of the students back to drive home the point that this type of group bullying would not be tolerated. In the end, though, the issue was not resolved and we went away that day feeling victimized. The best I could pry out of Christopher on the car ride home was that two influential students had convinced all the others to blame Christopher so that the team could get to the game on time. In response, I preached forgiveness to Christopher.

———————▼———————

Basketball season that year began with our latest coach making a bold prediction. He exclaimed that our team would win the state championship. His rationale was that our squad had a healthy first team back in action. From my point of view, it was a daring prediction coming from a person who was coaching eighth grade for the first time. It was difficult to find coaches willing to spend their free time working with grade school kids, and I knew we were lucky to have him as a coach, despite his lack of experience.

Unfortunately, his newbie status met squarely with Christopher's inability to manage his own emotions during the very first practice. Candidly, Jen and I knew managing emotions was the plight of many a Deaf person at this age. When they don't hear a message completely in social interactions, in a valiant attempt to fit in, a Deaf person will often just smile politely and bluff people into thinking they know what's going on. It's a coping device so that hearing people don't have to continually repeat the message to the Deaf person while the group of other listeners waits (sometimes impatiently) for the conversation to move forward. An even more volatile tangent of this is when the Deaf person thinks they heard something upsetting that may not even have been said. What comes forth is a series of emotional facial displays without any request for clarification. As parents of a Deaf child, we had attended many conference workshops on this subject.

At this first practice with the new coach, Christopher's team was down three points with fifty-eight seconds to go in a scrimmage. His coach began calling for the players to foul in order to stop the clock. That strategy didn't go over well with Christopher. In frustration, he put his head down and shook his head no. I happened to walk into the gym in time to see Christopher's reaction, and I understood what Christopher was thinking and trying to do. During this play, he and another player had trapped the opponent with the ball, and Christopher could see that a five-second call was coming. The offensive player had five seconds to either dribble, pass, or shoot or else the ball would go to Christopher's team. With that in mind, Christopher knew that fouling would be pointless. If he fouled his player, the opposition would be awarded free throws and the chance to expand the lead to five. Our coach, seeing that no one was listening to him, stopped the play and asked, "Why aren't you guys fouling?" When no one responded, the coach gave Christopher a bit of a tongue lashing for not following his directives. Christopher had played in fifty travel ball games over the summer, and the look on his face revealed how little confidence he had in his new coach.

The teachable moment was that sometimes a player could smile politely and respectfully follow a coach's plan even if he disagreed with it. While I did side with Christopher that the foul could have taken place with under thirty seconds on the clock and that there could have been a five-second call or turnover, I also talked to Christopher about not standing up to the coach in front of the other players. Christopher said back to me, "Dad, we had him and whatever he did next probably would be a turnover."

"What turnover?" I said.

Christopher responded, "We needed that five-second call!"

I informed Christopher that we were lucky to have our latest coach stepping up and volunteering and that the thing to do would have been for him to privately talk to the coach about his impressions of basketball strategy. I fully understood that this process was difficult for an eighth grader, but I wanted Christopher to know that these types of politics were everywhere. Additionally, Christopher wouldn't want his coach to think that he had a bad attitude.

After that rocky start, the eighth-grade fall basketball season was off and running. Our team's record was 2–0 in November. Christopher had been playing commendable basketball, especially in the areas of rebounding and scoring. The team's big rivalry game against the parochial school on the other side of town was coming up soon. Talk about Christopher being caught between two places. He attended one of the local parochial schools, but he was an altar boy at the rival's church. To further intensify this rivalry, Christopher had sealed the regional championship victory against this same team the year before when he hit two free throws with only seconds left to go in the game.

The gym was packed full the night of the game. I suppose it wasn't every day that a previous final four team from the state came to their place. The game was starting to look all ours as we took a five-point lead at the end of the first quarter. Unfortunately, Christopher committed two fouls and was benched for the remainder of the half. He didn't dig that at all, since his team was up by just one point at the half.

It was a different story in the second half. Christopher was a player possessed. When the smoke finally cleared at the end of the third period, our team was up by seventeen points. Christopher had snared ten rebounds and seven points in that quarter alone. Despite sitting out the second and fourth periods, he still finished the game with fourteen rebounds and made nine of his twelve free throws.

An interesting sidebar to the game was that a foursome of coaches from the local parochial high school had all shown up to watch the rivalry. One of those coaches caught me in the parking lot the following day and told me that it had been "eye popping" for our team to have beaten another respectable team by twenty-one points on their own court. "The other high school coaches thought pretty highly of Christopher, too," he said. "He was head and shoulders above the rest."

During the early games of the basketball season, Christopher's playing time averaged only a half of each game. I was reminded of the good old days when teams took care not to humiliate the other team when they were up by a large margin. Winning by forty would not be more of a victory, so everyone in for the second half was the way we rolled. I understood the philosophy, and as a father and former coach, I also was interested in seeing how Christopher would do once he began playing full games.

⎯⎯⎯▾⎯⎯⎯

Our team raced to a 14–0 start during Christopher's eighth-grade season, and I couldn't help but dream of what might be. At the same time, I wondered when the team might go flat. It had already nearly happened a couple of times over the season. Our guards had been revisiting some serious bad habits out on the court. The most prominent of these was dribbling with their heads down, and it was compounded by other bad habits. For years, four of the boys in the beginning lineup had relied on the full-court press defense to steal the ball and dribble to the basket in order to rack up points. The objective for these boys had been clear: ram it to the basket after the steal and either make the basket or draw a foul and get to the line. This strategy became problematic, however, when our team was in a tight game and we needed to get into a set offense. The good news was that most of the time when we ran the spread offense, the aggressive movement on the drive lanes to the goal had worked in our favor. Unfortunately, there had also been plenty of examples where a respectable defense had put our guards in situations where they either turned the ball over or took an off-balance shot.

The team's problem led me to contact one of the assistant coaches. He came from a basketball family and really knew the game. In fact, his father still held the single-game scoring record at our town's Big Ten school, and the apple didn't fall far from the tree. When we talked, the assistant coach completely agreed with my assessment of the team. "I brought up this same concern with the other coaches earlier this season," he explained, "but the message doesn't seem to be getting through." The other two coaches' sons were also the guards on the team. How could things change with that bias?

With that table set and no reasonable intervention, we lost the next two games in a row. One game was in overtime, and the other game was lost to the previous year's state champs. Our guards had difficulty recognizing the open area near our frontline guys. In the overtime game, Christopher had been so fed up with not getting the ball after the guards dribbled into a double-team trap that he rebounded their forced shots only to get fouled himself. Then, being so frustrated he didn't convert like he normally would have on his free throws. Christopher went five and thirteen from the line in that game, when he usually shot at seventy-five percent. His posture once again communicated how upset he was with the offense, and his inability to manage his own emotions once again prevailed.

Parents who coached their own kids rarely realized how much they overcompensated to give their kids the benefit of the doubt. As I watched one of Christopher's practices on a Saturday in January, I was amazed at how much bias I observed. One coach's son was leading the team in turnovers and was less than impressive with assists. The assist-to-turnover ratio per game is a commonly used statistic and is probably the best way to evaluate guards. Most coaches at this level would have taken a ratio of one-to-one. Our one guard easily had a one-to-two ratio. Because of this, Christopher took on the mission of sharing the rock as a way of demonstrating to our one guard, as well as a few other players, that we needed to move the ball around in order to stay out of traps and avoid turnovers.

As the team continued to work through its difficulties, the situation did improve. Christopher continued to average double-doubles, and his ball touches were way up as well. The coach who didn't have a son on the team continually asserted his will by saying, "Move the ball!" Who could complain?

We eased into the final portion of the season at 17–4, losing to our nemesis the defending AA state champion and three other much larger AAAA schools. Any coach who had seen our loss to the defending AA state champion would have agreed that the opposing team's guards had been exceptional. As a composite, their guards had an assist-to-turnover ratio of about three-to-one.

March Madness, or our February Frenzy at the grade school level, was fast approaching. One could only hope that the coaching parents would demonstrate less bias as the tournament progressed and the boys would continue to share the ball. I, for one, knew it would take extreme circumstances for me to coach Christopher. Like other dads out there, I thought way too highly of my own son and knew that coaching from that view would only lead to myopia.

In the meantime, the high school varsity coach was really looking forward to seeing Christopher in a year. Christopher now stood a little over six feet two inches tall, and he had plenty of growth left to go. The sky appeared to be the limit. As Christopher once said, "Brian Cook was six-foot-six when he was a high school freshman, and look what he accomplished."

Christopher grew up fast as his team primed itself for the state tournament. After considerable ongoing feedback from the non-parent coach, the boys were really sharing the ball better. Christopher was told to carry most of the scoring load, and he admirably responded. It was a good strategy, as Christopher had gone thirty out of thirty-seven from the floor during the team's last four games. That converted to just over eighty percent in shooting. Christopher had combined this with getting to the line, which was also a good sign. While he sometimes only played up to three quarters in these games, he still managed to maintain a double-digit rebounding average. That was a terrific stat to have before going into the tournament.

With all of Christopher's success, I admired how he kept his composure. This was an especially commendable feat during the regional tournament when he shot five for six from the floor and three for four from the line. He then gathered ten rebounds in just fifteen minutes of play. The line of students and community members waiting to congratulate him after the game was something to behold. Those who knew Christopher's history couldn't help but be emotionally supportive of the Deaf kid.

Later that week, our local parochial high school had an open house. It was a very well organized event, with all the teachers present to give tours of their respective areas. Toward the end of the evening, the players from the school's various sports teams were introduced in the gym. I could tell Christopher thought the academic component of the open house was just okay. For him, the real event that night took place in the gym. Afterward he marveled, "It's pretty cool the varsity players got to wear their uniforms." High school would soon be a reality.

The varsity players at the open house knew some of Christopher's history, and they challenged him to a game of horse off to the side in the school's main gym. As I was walking around the computer science area of the school after the game, I learned from one of the high school players that Christopher had outlasted four of the senior starters, losing only to the remaining point guard on the letter "e" in horse. I asked Christopher what the point guard's last shot was. He replied, "A runner." I wished we had practiced that!

———▼———

Back in state tournament play, who would have thought Christopher and his teammates would find themselves playing against the same team they had played the year before in the regional finals? Yes, our team's main competition was the other parochial school in town, which had dominated most of the boys' and girls' sports for years. The school's brand-new multimillion-dollar facility was a sight to see. The good news was that not only had our team outlasted them the prior year, but also our boys had defeated their team in basketball at least nine straight times in years past. As usual, the opposing team's fancy gym brought a large fan base. Our team, however, had the number one seed.

Christopher went into the game knowing the deal. He expected to be double- or even triple-teamed at times, and his goal was to then quickly get the ball to an open teammate. As it turned out, finding the open man would have worked perfectly if only our team had made its shots. As the game went on, it became clear that our players were shooting some prayers. From my seat in the stands, I wondered if the basketball gods were with our team that night. How could we win if we were only shooting twenty percent from the floor?

During a poignant moment near the end of the game, our non-parent coach pulled Christopher off to the sideline.

"I want you to take it to the rack every time. Understand? Even if you're double-teamed," he said.

That seemed kind of desperate to me but his words resonated with Christopher. His team was down by two points with just seconds left in the game. Our opponents had upcoming free throws, but fortunately for us, they missed them. We then took a timeout with exactly ten seconds left on the clock. After the timeout, the ball swung a little to the right. Christopher received the inside pass and quickly spun around for a seven-foot jump shot. Believe it or not, the shot came up short. Incredibly, Christopher rebounded again for a quick shot that took a funny bounce before he finally tipped it in with little time left. Thanks to that move, our team earned overtime. It took two overtimes, with a big basket by the coach's son and Christopher shooting clutch free throws, to outlast the opposing team.

After that hard-fought victory in the regional finals, Christopher's team was set to play for the sectional championship in a small town in the southern portion of our state. This town was known by most as a mecca for basketball. Luckily for us, their powerhouse grade school had already been defeated. This meant our team would go up against another strong team that was from an area thirty miles east of us.

The game itself was tight. Christopher took over late in the contest with a number of key plays and rebounds. During the game, I noticed that a few of the other team's teen fans were mimicking some of the signs I made to Christopher on the floor. The teens made comments such as, "Peace," when I signaled the number two to Christopher. Whenever I signaled to Christopher to keep his hands up, they yelled, "Touchdown!" It actually did not concern me too much at first. These signals from the stands really helped Christopher, since inevitably his back was turned or his view obstructed when the coach tried to signal him. Our goal was to make sure that Christopher knew exactly what the plan was from the bench. As the game continued, our team took more control, and I sensed the teen fans' growing frustration. The mocking intensified. That's when I walked over to one of the boys to deliver a message. "Hey, I saw what you were doing. I must look pretty silly signing to my Deaf son." Well, one would have thought I was speaking in another language. The response was silence. While walking away, I heard the teen share my information with his mom, who scoffed at the sensitivity of my message. Christopher's team won the game, and I was more than happy to move on.

From that game, Christopher's team traveled northwest to participate in elite eight state championship play. It was fun for the team to be back at the elite eight for its second year in a row. Christopher's height had been nearly five feet ten inches during the previous season, but he had grown a good four inches since then. His new height had our school hoping for great things.

In the initial matchup, our team drew a representative from the far southern portion of our state. Right from the start, the crowd could see that both teams were nervous. Christopher, however, was right at his usual pace for a double-double as our team pulled ahead sixteen to twelve.

The second half of the game was heart-stopping as the lead went back and forth. With about a minute left to play, Christopher drove the ball to put our team up by two. In turn, our opponent quickly scored and tied the game. There were just nineteen seconds left, and our team's intent was to hold the ball so Christopher could take the last shot. To our dismay, the opponent disrupted our team's play by intentionally fouling. Their team thought this tactic would work, and it did. Our guard missed the first part of a one-and-one, which led to our opponent shooting the winning basket. After the game, the other team's fans approached Christopher and commented on how gracious he had been during his final grade school game. Christopher took the same position I did: his team had played hard, but the other team deserved to win on a very bold strategic move that on this afternoon went their way.

Christopher and I didn't take much time off at the end of that season. Instead, we headed to the Chicago area for AAU travel ball tryouts just one week later. This group was run by a former Midwest Big Ten university basketball player. Two tryouts had already taken place in February, but Christopher hadn't been able to attend either one since they had both been scheduled during his grade school state championship. I emailed the Fourteen U team coach to let him know that Christopher was interested in trying out. Thankfully, the coach saw something in Christopher's bio that put us on the road soon after.

Hours later, we arrived at a mega-church in the Chicago suburbs for the tryout. After Christopher's tryout, the coach came over and spoke with us for about twenty minutes. He stated that Christopher had a "unique skill set" and that his "up side" was something they were excited about for their team. "As far as we're concerned, Christopher has made the team. Now it's up to him to decide if he wants to join us," he said. We were flattered by the offer. Once the coach answered our play signing and summer schedule questions, we paid the fee and signed up. It was to be another new beginning for Christopher.

Travel ball lived up to its name. Every Tuesday and Thursday around 4:00 p.m. Christopher and I left town and drove to the Chicago area for his two-hour-long practice. If we were lucky, we would return home from our three-hundred-mile round trip by midnight. The positive side to our travel time was that Christopher easily had two hours to complete his homework as well as catch some sleep in the car. He was continuing his pattern of academic excellence in school and we wanted nothing to interfere with that.

The AAU tournaments mostly took place on Saturdays and Sundays, so our family was able to stay home and relax in our hometown each Friday. Then we were off to Chicago or some other city in the Midwest for the weekend.

The AAU talent was exceptional as usual. Our Fourteen U team placed second in one of the early tournaments. It was obvious that all the young guns on our team had been special players back at their respective grade schools. Further, the players' parents were very involved and quickly scurried from gym to gym in a valiant effort to watch their sons play. With innate athleticism and years of practice, the kids on the AAU team simply played harder and faster than other grade school players. They had a "take no prisoners, playing for keeps" mentality as well. It was a winning system. Even the players' parents exclusively hung out with each other.

Christopher's AAU team either won or was a finalist in many of the tournaments within our state. All of the players were excellent at the Fourteen U level. The only time our team was outmatched was when the big teams from the other states participated and some truly phenomenal players began asserting their will.

Given our team's current level of competition, just having more wins than losses was considered good. The double-double games were few and far between, but Christopher got his first one that April against some very tough competition. I noticed the AAU refs tended to let a lot of calls go. I asked one of the refs what the intent of this was, and he told me it was to prepare some of the incoming freshmen for their high school varsity teams. With that kind of refereeing, AAU ball had a level of roughness that sometimes resembled street ball. To some extent, it was probably good for Christopher to experience this type of play, so he could learn to become a bit more physical himself.

During that same spring, Christopher started to work out with the local high school coach before and after school. After the first workout, the coach gave me a report. "Your son is very talented. It'll be difficult to keep him off of the varsity team," he said. This was high praise for a fourteen-year-old, and it gave our family something to ponder. On one hand, it was good to see that the coach believed in Christopher and acknowledged his skill set, but on the other hand, we knew that it might not be the best idea for Christopher to be socially disconnected from his freshman peer group. We would just have to wait and see where the cards fell.

Christopher continued with his AAU team on Tuesdays and Thursdays, and he worked out with some very talented players at the local Boys and Girls Club on Wednesday evenings. His weekends were usually filled with AAU games. On the rare Saturday and Sunday off of AAU, Christopher privately trained using a custom program that had been designed by a family friend who was also a former college basketball coach. All in all, it was a very busy spring, and soon we were making plans for the summer. The year before, Christopher had attended ten summer camps, but the summer of 2010 would be spent working out with his high school team and playing AAU ball. In between games he would be taking an Intro to Driver's Ed class and an online math course to help him get ahead. It would be another full summer.

———▾———

Before summer even officially started, basketball parents at the high school were asked to sign their kids up for the level of team they thought their sons should play for during summer league that June. We could choose the freshman, junior varsity, or varsity team. This was an easy task for the parents of juniors and seniors, but it wasn't so easy for our family, since Christopher was fourteen and an incoming freshman. We had been told that Christopher had the skill to play on either the junior varsity or the varsity team. The problem was that Christopher weighed in at a mere one hundred and fifty pounds, and Jen and I had concerns about his strength compared to the older boys. We ended up not signing him up for a team. Instead, we left it up to the coach to place Christopher where he thought was best. Imagine our surprise when Christopher was assigned to the freshman, junior varsity, and varsity teams!

The high school summer league games came in reverse order, with the varsity team in action first. Christopher had the unenviable task of covering a regional all-state player during the first game. The next week he played in a different part of the state against another preseason all-state player. As I watched him play at this level, there was no doubt in my mind that he needed to be physically stronger to compete.

Christopher did, nevertheless, look like an all-state player at the freshman level, and he more than held his own against the competition at the junior varsity level. In fact, it was pretty obvious that he was one of the top JV players. That said, I thought that if he continued to play hard, he could probably earn a jersey for the varsity team. I had to admit that it would be quite an accomplishment for him to letter as a freshman on the varsity team.

In one tournament in Indiana, Christopher spent three days playing plenty of basketball. The games were very quick, fifteen-minute running clock halves that led to a lot of games. In just one day, Christopher played in ten total JV and varsity games. On the final day of the tournament, he suffered a back injury and had to sit out. The varsity team ended up pulling out of the tournament due to its number of injured players, but the junior varsity team went 13–1 to win the championship.

There was no rest for the weary from then on out. Christopher rejoined AAU ball as soon as July began. Unfortunately, he reinjured his spine during his first day of practice. He fell to the floor that night and for the first time ever could not get up. That's when Jen and I decided Christopher needed a medical consultation. We also made the decision for him to take a break from AAU during the month of July.

I suppose I should have seen it coming. The long eighth-grade basketball season, AAU, and intense high school summer ball condensed into June had all contributed to Christopher being diagnosed in August with a very serious stress fracture of the third lumbar vertebrae. It made total sense to me, and I realized that players shouldn't attempt to play through serious injuries. Many novice high school coaches tended to push their players to play through their injury pain, but that only leads to further injury.

If any good news came from Christopher's injury, it was that his x-rays confirmed that his growth plates were wide open. This meant he still had some more growing to do after he healed from his fracture. Sadly, though, Christopher would not be able to play basketball for at least two months.

CHAPTER 8

THE SIX-TWO FRESHMAN

———————▼———————

With Christopher's spine still on the mend, I questioned my own judgment in having let him play so much basketball in such a condensed period of time. Had the excessive basketball playing led to his stress fracture? Could genetics have played a role? *How had this happened?* These questions swirled around in my head, but the end result remained the same. If I was to guess, Christopher had probably gradually broken his spine while playing in some rough AAU games at the end of May. In late June, he played those ten abbreviated-clock high school games in one day, and his spine must have just given out.

A friend of mine—a former college coach—agreed to help Christopher with his rehabilitation. His plan was to first stabilize Christopher's core in order to reduce the stress on the spine itself. Luckily for Christopher, spending the remainder of his summer in an itchy brace wasn't too life changing, and he would be out of the brace and in full rehabilitation by late September. But until then Christopher had to just step back and relax. With a new high school starting soon, there was definitely plenty to do academically.

Christopher's first year of high school started off well. He appeared to fit in with his classmates, and the administration seemed open to accommodating his specialized needs. It wasn't until a while later that my wife and I noticed the school had become disagreeable with making the requested accommodations for Christopher's disability.

As a Deaf person, Christopher had to work harder mentally than other students and could become exhausted from too much information coming his way all day long. To help him through the intense school day, we requested for Christopher to have a second study hall. He had taken a summer math course, and with that, we knew he would have plenty of credits to appropriately complete his first school year. We also knew that, without an extra study hall break, he would be worn out from attempting to attentively listen in such a rigorous academic environment. Two strategically placed study halls would do wonders to break up his school day. But the school pushed back. I wish I could say that their opposition was based on policy or a philosophy they had that was somewhat valid. Instead, the reasoning was that they had never done two study halls for anyone before, so to be consistent they could not permit this for Christopher. As an academic professional myself, I had planned for Christopher to essentially go to school year-round from here on out in preparation for college, as the ability to spread the course work out would benefit him very well given his disability. But the school wouldn't budge. Once again we were in a stare-down.

As a last-ditch attempt, I tried to break things down for the administration. I said, "Let's say you are an international student with some commendable English skills. You are not good at understanding at one hundred percent but can grasp about seventy percent of what people are saying. The good news is that last year you were actually at fifty percent, so that trajectory is great and with a good pace over the next couple years the goal would be one hundred percent. However, the pace is the key. Listening and figuring things out with language is hard work. You definitely don't want to pack too much into a short period of time like the first semester of high school in an already rigorous academic environment. A more effective plan—especially if the student already earned credit in the summer applied to the first year—would be to pace oneself. The ideal plan on a given day then would be to take a few classes, then have study hall to review what you heard and understood and what you may have missed. After the study hall, you could try another couple classes, then take a break for lunch. The afternoon then would be simply a division of class and one remaining study hall." I thought that this example would put things in proper perspective and they would see why our request was essential to Christopher's academic achievement. To my dismay, they remained unconvinced.

So there we were again down the same old road with Jen and me saying here is what we want to have regarding accommodations and the school administrators having their own view. Candidly, it brought back very bad memories of when we had been at similar impasses in the past. We had learned that we had to seek legal counsel.

I believe that this time around Christopher's school was just plain unable to help us. At a meeting with the principal, he mentioned without even thinking that "sometimes with accommodations like extended time for testing you just have to call it because no matter how much additional time was given, the outcome will probably be the same." If this is the philosophy of the leader of the school, I thought, then how could the necessary accommodations be implemented by the staff and teachers? Our periodic meetings with staff, teachers, and the administration were rarely more productive. When Jen and I would suggest basic accommodations such as an alternate testing area for Christopher, select personnel in the school acted like this was unduly burdensome. Jen and I often left in disbelief at the lack of understanding, and frankly we didn't look forward to the periodic meetings.

Christopher's high school basketball team tryout was coming up later in the fall, and we thought he most likely would not be playing on the freshman team. With good rehab on his spine, we wondered if he would be on the junior varsity or varsity team. As fall continued on in all its splendor, we saw Christopher put his basketball concerns on the back burner. He decided to take a big risk and ask the prettiest girl in his class to the homecoming dance.

It seemed as though his wait to ask her went on for weeks, as he wanted to pop the question at just the perfect time. I found myself swept up in all the homecoming drama as well. At Jen's request, I even called the girl's mom to scope out whether it was a good idea for Christopher to ask her daughter to the dance. The mom, who worked in one of the academic offices I was familiar with, told me yes, and she invited Christopher over to their house that night to ask. Christopher got all dolled up and I drove him to the girl's house for the big event. I told him I would wait in the car until he had finished asking. I watched as he cautiously exited the car while holding his invitation and choc-olate-dipped strawberries. He then slowly walked up to her front door. Five minutes later he was back.

"She said yes!" he announced.

I tried to be cool and not ask him too many questions, but I had distinctly heard the screams coming from inside the house as he left. "So tell me what happened."

"Well, it was kind of hard to get the question out since her mom and sisters were eavesdropping and kind of peeking around the corners from room to room in the house."

"I can see where that would be distracting."

"Yeah. And then, after she said yes, I heard cheering from the other room."

"Is that right? I'd say it was worth taking the chance then, don't you think?"

As we quietly drove home, Christopher received a gracious text from his fu-ture homecoming date. She thanked him and also apologized for her "crazy" family members.

I didn't want Christopher's first date to be too stressful for him. I couldn't help but wonder if his date would accept and appreciate him for who he was, given his hearing issues. As I understood it from Christopher, they hadn't spent a whole lot of time to-gether, so she might not be used to everything. Overall, though, I was very happy that his future date had been nice to him, and I hoped she was truly interested in going to the dance with him. I did not consider myself to be a high school dance expert by any means, but I did believe that the students who were fixated on attending the dances as couples would soon learn that things were seriously overrated.

There probably weren't too many families who practiced taking pictures, but we did. Christopher's facial paralysis had never been completely addressed and it had start-ed to affect his self-esteem. That night before his dance, we happily put in a thirty-min-ute photography session to help Christopher find his best smile. In the end, he had mastered a wry-looking smile that was pretty darn good!

The night of the homecoming dance, Christopher was in good shape. I was the chauffeur, and we arrived right on time. He gave his date her corsage, and the two of them had their pictures taken at her house before they headed off to a nice dinner and then the dance. Afterward, Christopher and his date, along with a few other couples, returned to our house for Ping-Pong and arcade games. At the end of the night, her mom came by to pick her up and I found myself supervising a hug session at our front door before Christopher's date left to go home.

Christopher was up fairly early the next day and I for one was most curious as to how things had gone with the dance the evening before. I decided the best posture was to let him bring it up. He was growing like a weed at that time, so I just kept shoveling more food his way to extend our potential interaction. Just as I got tired of talking about the weather and family plans for the remainder of the weekend, he spilled. "Dinner last night was good, but I didn't say much. The restaurant was kind of noisy. But the dance was fun."

"Oh, and did you dance much?" Jen asked.

"Some. She had to dance on her tiptoes just to reach my shoulders." He smiled. Jen and I were happy to hear it had been so amicable.

A week later Christopher asked his homecoming date out again, but she said she was busy. Christopher hoped that wasn't the end of things, but after some cold interactions with her in the hallway, he finally understood her subtle rejection. Later, when he saw her talking to his buddy a lot more than she had ever spoken to him, Christopher was hurt. It was difficult for me to see him in a state of wishing things could be different.

He found me in the living room not much later. "Hey, Dad, can I ask you something?"

"Of course. What have you got for me?"

"Did this ever happen to you before you met Mommy?"

"You mean a girl suddenly deciding she likes someone else? Sure. It hurts, I know."

"What do I do now?" he asked.

I said, "You know, I think it's time to take a step back and gain some perspective. She knows who you are and where to find you if you two need to talk."

"But, Dad," he said, "what if she is too shy and doesn't want to look silly making the move my way?"

"Give it some time and see how things go with you not initiating."

"Well, if she really wanted to go out I think she would actually find a way to work it out, right?"

"That's right." I was impressed he had come to this conclusion on his own. I added, "The best advice I can give you is to not take it personally or dwell on the negative. Just be there for her as a friend."

Christopher walked away and my heart went out to him. It was difficult to see him struggling that way. Then the unexpected happened. One fall day a few weeks later I was relaxing at home when, out of the blue, I received an email from the mom of Christopher's homecoming date. The message said she thought it would be a good idea for her daughter to join our family in volunteering on Saturdays at the Swann Center, the local residential center that helped young people with disabilities. I was stunned. Christopher was confused, yet something in me said to give the girl another chance. Several emails later the volunteer plans were finally arranged.

The girl arrived at our house around noon the next Saturday. Unfortunately, she was too late to volunteer with us. While she was very pleasant to all of us, she was quiet. As a nice gesture, and knowing her entire family liked the chocolate-covered strawberries he gave her before, Christopher gave her a card and some cookie dough to congratulate her for making both the junior varsity and varsity high school basketball teams as a freshman.

The two of them later took in a football game and then played a little basketball outside our house. When it was time for the young woman to leave, Christopher gave her his customary hug and watched her walk away with her card and cookie dough. I couldn't help but wonder how she would treat Christopher at school. Would she give him the less interactive mode the next time she saw him? I certainly hoped not, for Christopher's sake. He clearly enjoyed her company a great deal. Only time would tell.

—————▼—————

The beginning of Christopher's first high school basketball season arrived. For the last few weeks Christopher had been working hard at stabilizing his core and doing some light cardio workouts on a stationary bike now that his brace was off. He had been watching the high school team play since he was in the fifth grade, and now it was finally his turn on the court.

The coach initially placed Christopher with his freshman peers for workouts. The practices ran from 6:00 to 7:30 a.m. This gave him just enough time to shower and get to class. Our family was surprised that Christopher started out with the freshmen since he had AAU basketball experience. We supposed that a formal tryout would be the one way the coaches could insulate Christopher from accusations of favoritism if and when they decided to move him up to the next level. There were fifteen spots available on the freshman team, but counting Christopher, there were twenty young men trying out to play.

It didn't take too long for things to settle out. Just one week later, Christopher was moved up to play with the junior varsity team. Two weeks after that, the coaches informed him that he would also dress with the varsity team but would continue to play with the JV team as well. Later that month, he got into his first varsity tournament and scored. We were all thrilled to see his name listed in the tournament program as a ninth grader. Most of the other players were eleventh and twelfth graders. Additionally, Christopher was playing some good JV basketball. After two games, he was averaging a double-double just like the old days.

The upcoming holiday tournament was going to be a big deal, since the Fighting Illini, our state's Big Ten team, was hosting it. Teams from all around would come to play, and our family was looking forward to seeing the competition during the one-day event. Even better, when the day of the tournament arrived, Christopher played good minutes under the big lights. He actually got in the box score with three rebounds. Afterward, he told Jen and me that one of the recruiters from U of I had caught him in the tunnel before his game and wished him well. Christopher, of course, told the recruiter that he wasn't sure how much playing time he would get, but the coach responded that Christopher's time would soon come. I reflected on that thought, wondering once again about how Christopher's whole basketball journey would play out. At the moment, though, Christopher was preoccupied with the girl he had taken to the homecoming dance. She had gone to the arena with us and watched his game. Life was good for him!

CHAPTER 9

---▼---

Besides the tournament, December also brought Christopher's first round of high school final exams. His ten-hour-long study days right before exam week seemed to have paid off, as the results put him on the honor roll. We were proud of him in the way he was able to meet such a challenge at a school that was less than accommodating. He didn't know it yet, but Jen and I planned on giving him and his new female friend a surprise day trip to Chicago once finals were over as a reward for all that hard work.

It was still unclear to me whether Christopher's new friend was really interested in him. I felt perhaps she didn't yet understand how to interact with Christopher as a friend, much less as a boyfriend. I initially thought that communicating with the girl's mother was the best way to facilitate their interaction. But I had noticed that the mother's emails to me had slowed, and after a brief resurgence, her daughter had once again become less attentive to Christopher. I had a gut feeling that she might not be digging our son as much as we did.

I could sympathize with those who didn't know how to handle another person's different needs. I had always been a bit ashamed of an encounter I had with one of my daughter's young friends. One day our family invited a boy from Rachel's first-grade class over to our home for a playdate. While the day had been our daughter's idea, it was obvious to us it would be a challenge for us to accommodate her friend's needs. Rachel's friend was in a wheelchair, and we quickly learned that there were things we could and couldn't do with him. Board games, talking, and TV were all good activities, but outdoor activities were mostly off limits since we thought it would be insensitive for him to watch our daughter run around and play on our uneven grass while he was confined to his chair on our patio. As the afternoon went on, I watched as Rachel's playmate got frustrated over his needs. He was struggling to connect with us as well. Looking back on that day, I felt bad that I had overwhelmed him with so many questions about what he wanted to do. The result was that he became increasingly quiet and ultimately shut down.

Over the years, I had given a lot of thought to that experience. The word *ephphatha*, which originates from the Aramaic language dating back nearly three thousand years, is found in the Bible just once. It means "be opened." In the spirit of *ephphatha*, I wished I had demonstrated an ability simply to work with and accept Rachel's friend's challenges. Had I done so, I think I would have been a more patient and tolerant person on that day. Given this experience, I hoped and prayed that Christopher's new life acquaintances would be opened to accepting him as well.

———▼———

Over winter break, Christopher was focused on getting a little more varsity playing time on the hardwood. His coach, however, was very concerned that he still wasn't strong enough. Christopher had worked out with the second-string varsity team before the start of the season, but now that the season had officially begun, the coach had him on the third-string rotation. Being on the third string meant that Christopher had to watch more than he played, which allowed him to learn but did not do much to make him stronger.

Christopher was again in somewhat of a catch-22: he wanted to get stronger, but he wasn't able to do much weight training since he was still growing so quickly. I counseled him to focus on what he needed to improve on in order to catch the coach's eye. Playing hard and looking to score, rebound, and share the ball were things that had and would continue to serve him well.

Partway through the season, Christopher suddenly began signaling for the coach to take him out as early as the third quarter of the JV games. Initially, the coach thought Christopher was just spent and needed a rest. This happened in four games over the course of a two-week period. Then, the coaches noticed that Christopher's finishing spot on the practice running drills had dropped by about twenty-five percent. When he developed a morning cough that would not go away until after eight o'clock each day, we knew we had a problem.

Jen and I could hardly imagine what might be causing these symptoms. Christopher had always been so athletic, with endless stamina. This was the same kid who had lapped his teammates at soccer practice and outlasted high school guys in the pacer test. What was going on?

It took two trips to the doctor and a handful of tests to finally get a diagnosis: exercise-induced asthma. The doctor prescribed Christopher an inhaler, and he showed improvement.

As I watched Christopher struggle with yet another medical device, I wondered how much more he could take. To further compound things, Christopher had also badly injured his thumb while playing. Thankfully the doctor didn't find a break, and he was back to his normal self a week later.

———▼———

Christopher had always been a thinker, and now at age fifteen he decided to conduct an experiment. He was still very much interested in having his homecoming date become something more. She had accepted his invitation for a day trip to Chicago with our family, and she had also attended his New Year's Eve party. He had really enjoyed her company, but he had also noticed he was always the one doing the initiating. What would happen if he waited for her to ask *him* to do something?

He took a piece of paper and drew two columns. The first column he labeled "Things I Did" and the second column he labeled "Things She Did." Then he wrote down all of their interactions up to that time and over the next two weeks. When Dr. Christopher tallied the results, there were a whopping twenty-eight hours in his column and only fifteen minutes in hers.

A sad reality set in for Christopher after his experiment ended. He wouldn't be contacting her anymore. He was visibly shaken by this fact, and he struggled with how to relay his concerns to her. Talking with her was out of the question, as he was simply too nervous around her now. After processing it all, Christopher decided to share his thoughts with her in a written note. The ball would then be in her court one last time. Unfortunately, there was no response from her. Nothing. It was a tough end but we knew Christopher would get through it.

———•———

In February of 2011, Christopher found a new male role model whom he described to Jen and me as "way cool." Michael Lizarraga was the only Deaf college basketball player competing in a Division I program. He lived in California, and his story had been featured on CBS and ESPN. Christopher had read about Michael's squad making the NCAA tournament as kind of a Cinderella team and he wanted to meet him. One contact led to another and soon the two young men were emailing each other.

The boys had a great rapport. Both had been born Deaf, although only Christopher had a cochlear implant. Michael was a signer, whereas Christopher utilized spoken language. Christopher questioned his new buddy about basketball strategies and the best ways to communicate with teammates and coaches. Michael wanted to know how well Christopher's implant had been working for him. Michael was also a positive academic role model. It was a blessing to have him in Christopher's life.

One of the most exciting things to happen to Christopher as a young teenager transpired soon after he met Michael. One day, the administrative assistant at my work handed me a phone message from a woman named Dana O'Neil. The message said she worked at ESPN and wanted to talk to me about Christopher. Before returning the woman's call, I decided to do a quick computer search of her position at ESPN. I discovered that her role in college basketball couldn't have been any higher. She had recently interviewed and written an article about the future number one NBA draft pick who was just about to come out of a top-ranked college basketball program. I picked up the phone.

Dana was very formal and had obviously done her homework. She said, "Dr. Caulfield, I was talking to Michael Lizarraga, who as you probably know is the only Deaf person playing men's basketball in Division I NCAA competition."

I replied, "Oh, yes, Michael and my son Christopher know each other."

"That's what I understand. Michael has indicated that if I really wanted to talk to a young, upcoming player who has dreams to play in college that I should contact Christopher Caulfield." She added, "I want to tell the story about how he came to be friends with Michael Lizarraga."

"That sounds great. Let me give you Christopher's cell number and you can just talk to him."

There was a moment of silence on the phone and then Dana said, "Oh, I thought I would be working with an interpreter to communicate with Christopher."

I said, "Nah, he is a big talker."

She said she would call Christopher the following day. We hung up then. I was stunned. I could hardly wait to tell Christopher.

The article appeared on ESPN.com and was very nicely done. O'Neil ultimately interviewed me, Jen, Christopher, Michael, and both of Michael's parents. It was striking how much our two families had in common. We had experienced nearly the exact same emotionally intense journey through diagnosis, acceptance, education, and a love of basketball. In one quote near the end of the article, Christopher summed up how much his friendship with Michael meant to him.

"Throughout my whole life, I thought I was the only deaf kid who was playing basketball," Christopher said. "I thought about playing in college, but I didn't think I could. I thought I wouldn't fit in. It was very hard. Now I think I'm like everybody else. I just have certain challenges. I just have to step up like Michael did and beat my disability. He can do it. So can I."

With as thrilling as it was to have that interview published, we never expected all the attention that soon followed. A prominent university from out east read the article and invited Christopher to attend its leadership conference that summer. The media in our town also loved the story. One network wanted to send a reporter to interview Christopher's coaches, parents, and friends on the high school gym floor. A second local media station wanted to interview our family and talk about how Christopher turned out to be such a great basketball player as well as a strong student athlete. The network reporters were also very interested in hearing about his impact on the community. For years, Christopher had been involved with the Boys and Girls Club and the school for the Deaf in our area. Even more amazing to the media was that he had spent almost every Saturday he was available for the past seven years at the Swann Center, volunteering with disabled children.

The media's love affair with Christopher didn't end there. Local television reporters even followed him to his regional championship game that winter. One reporter, Ashley Sears, was especially interested in pursuing the human interest story. Although Christopher wouldn't be playing in that varsity regional game as a freshman, the television cameras still focused on him warming up, sitting on the bench, and supporting his teammates. The cameras also captured Jen and me sitting on the bleachers and cheering for Christopher's squad. It was amazing to see all of this attention focused on a kid who had overcome some very serious obstacles in his life.

It wasn't all about the cameras in that tournament. During the final game of regionals, I learned yet another profound and emotional lesson about human nature. In the heat of the game, a referee missed our coach's timeout request. The result was a turnover by our squad, and our fan base went crazy. Sadly, the crowd directed endless names such as "Idiot" and "Dummy" at the referee. Then came the "D" bomb. "What are you, DEAF?" The crowd continued to berate the referee with at least four rounds of hateful speech. Needless to say, my wife and I sat there feeling humiliated and stunned after hearing the "D" bomb shouted. As the two of us sat motionless on the bleachers, I had a funny feeling that the others standing around us had finally started putting two and two together. I saw family members nudging others and whispering to the shouters that they should stop. It was a disgrace at an otherwise exciting game. Christopher's team went on to upset the number one team to win the regional championship.

I experienced a wide array of emotions while reflecting on Christopher's first year of high school basketball. Who would have thought a varsity team with an under-.500 record could have won the regional title? Along the way, Christopher had also played enough quarters to earn a varsity letter as a freshman. Our family proudly enjoyed attending the end-of-season basketball banquets.

In addition, at that year's AAU ceremony, Christopher was recognized as being a model teammate. One of the AAU coaches there praised him for having been the most unselfish player on the basketball floor that season. So much to be grateful for!

———•———

Our family traveled to Los Angeles over spring break for a well-deserved vacation. We toured Hollywood, took a day trip to Anaheim to watch Duke practice for its Sweet Sixteen appearance, and even stopped at the *Queen Mary* in Long Beach. But for as much fun as those adventures were, one of the real highlights was Christopher and Michael getting to meet in person at Michael's university. During our visit, we toured one of the university's centers that support the Deaf students on campus. After all our family's struggles with the educational system, it was nice for us to see that there was a place on campus that supported students with disabilities and made accommodations for them. In this college's case, a wealthy donor had supplied the school with the funding to make the center a reality.

Back home, our family heeded the varsity basketball coach's advice for Christopher to become stronger. I once again appealed to a colleague of mine for help. A former college basketball coach, he had previously helped Christopher rehab from his spinal stress fracture. He graciously developed another workout plan that would help Christopher continue to strengthen his core and better support his lumbar spine as well as build some overall muscle mass. A by-product of this intense workout was weight gain. As time went on, Christopher was happy about the observable changes taking place with his appearance.

I hadn't realized it before, but Christopher's diet was also vital to his training. His overall eating plan was to consume plenty of calories in order to build more body mass before summer basketball began. His hope was that, by gaining more strength, he would really surprise people when he returned to the gym. Jen and I were amazed at how quickly our grocery bill had escalated!

Now halfway through Christopher's second semester of high school, Jen and I once again evaluated Christopher's academic progress. To that point, his performance had been top-notch. We weren't as sure about the school's performance, however. We had received some mixed messages from the administration regarding Christopher's accommodations, and it was our opinion that a less than diverse staff had led in part to too much like-mindedness. The school's teaching emphasis was concentrated on those students in the middle or mean area. The bright students seemed to be self-sustaining, so the teachers did not focus too much energy on them. On the opposite end of the bell curve were the needy students. These were the ones I felt for the most due to their vulnerability. Christopher was a kind of hybrid. He definitely needed to have the playing field leveled with essential accommodations, but once those accommodations were in place, he was ready to soar. Our view was that only when the accommodations were managed and applied effectively would Christopher be able to achieve his best. Like us, Christopher was getting frustrated over disagreements regarding accommodations. We needed to make a change.

With this in mind, Jen and I began contemplating a three-year high school plan for Christopher. We talked about it one night before bed.

"He has already been moving ahead with his earned credits, and he is planning to take summer school. I think he'll be able to handle it," I said to Jen.

"I know." She folded her arms. "It will be a lot, but if he plays basketball in college, he will have that time to slow things down."

"That's right. If he makes the team, he will most likely redshirt. He just won't be strong enough by the time he's seventeen. Doing five years in college will easily counterbalance the three years in high school."

We discussed the plan with Christopher, and he was intrigued by the idea. As we put our plan on paper, it became clear that Christopher would need to start taking dual credit courses at our community college immediately. While this would be a change in environment for him, he would earn additional credits that he could apply to college. After a few revisions, the plan was set. The beauty of our plan was that it wouldn't be binding for a while. Christopher would have nine and a quarter total credits after the upcoming summer. His high school required twenty-three and three-quarters credits to graduate. With a little work, he could complete the remaining fifteen or so credits in two years.

At the same time, I constructed a basketball pull-out strategy in my head just in case Christopher's past spinal injury came back to hinder his play. I didn't want to alarm Christopher, but I wanted any such changes to be as smooth as possible, should the need arise. Given all that Christopher had achieved in basketball, I wondered how he would adjust to that potential change.

In some ways it seemed Christopher was at a fork in the road. His situation reminded me of a terrific student athlete I had known back when he was a college freshman and I was an academic professional. He had been recruited by a number of Division II schools; however, in the end, he realized basketball was a short-term opportunity for him. His real love was health care, so he started his education, minus a basketball scholarship, at a community college. I had been so impressed by his courage in walking away from all that had athletically defined him before college. Tragically, he died one day at just nineteen years old while playing basketball just for fun. The news stunned both me and his other student friends. We collected donations to help his family and planted a tree in his honor. I still think of him and his courage to "be opened" to taking the path less followed every Arbor Day.

At the end of Christopher's school year, our family planned another trip to Chicago to reward him for his outstanding academic achievements. Jen and I gave Christopher the opportunity to invite a friend to go along on our trip. To our surprise, he wanted to ask a new girl. I once again chose the secure path and called the girl's dad, who was an acquaintance of mine. If it wasn't cool with him or the mom, we would graciously take a step away from the invite. By the end of the day, her dad had already called back and given us his permission.

Christopher's new friend, C.D., was a bit of a track star, to say the least. She, like Christopher, had earned a varsity letter in her sport when she was just a freshman. Jen and I really enjoyed how she was genuinely interested in Christopher's life. The only source of rivalry between the two teenagers was that C.D. was a huge fan of U of I and Christopher was loyal to Duke. I instructed Christopher to be cool about his Blue Devil conversations with her.

I'm not sure I would have called this trip to Chicago a date, but things couldn't have gone more smoothly that day. Jen and I couldn't help but notice a number of great things about C.D. One was that she was an expert communicator. As Christopher put it, "She communicates with a purpose." This was good because, at age fifteen, Christopher needed to be around people who talked a bit. A bonus was that his friend's voice was not so meek that she couldn't be heard.

During our day trip, we all stopped for lunch, and the conversation was excellent there as well. In the afternoon we attended the Blue Man Group, which the kids especially enjoyed, then we headed to the lake front to rent tandem bikes. I warned C.D. that she should be the front person on the tandem given Christopher's hearing loss. It was a bit challenging, but after switching things up a bit, we all had a fun experience. We wrapped up the evening with dinner downtown at the Grand Lux Café. We had a great meal and legendary desserts. On the drive home, my wife and I agreed we couldn't have asked for a better day.

Christopher's relationships were full of hits and misses as he attempted to interact with his hearing peers. After the Chicago trip, he unfortunately found himself in the same boat with this female friend as he had been with the other girls he had been interested in. When he asked C.D. out again, she was "busy." Jen and I hoped that Christopher did not get his confidence too broken along this path. Our prayer was that he would meet someone who was right for him.

Spurred on by the ESPN story from earlier in the year, the local media once again contacted our family in the summer of 2011. The reporters wanted to explore all of the groups involved in helping Christopher become who he was. Our family was thrown into full access mode again. When the news piece finally aired, the most telling comment was, "When you see this story, you immediately find it hard not to cry and smile at the same time." Another person said, "Someone should write a book about this kid." Christopher wasn't invited to many parties, and he didn't go on many dates, but the media loved him.

It was about this same time when things started getting even more emotionally difficult for Christopher in high school. He was becoming most concerned with the paralysis on the left side of his face. My wife and I decided that it was again time to have a consultation with a doctor about it. We began to search for a nerve specialist who could give us some renewed hope for Christopher's facial symmetry. In Christopher's case, the upper portion of his left lip was not completely elevating, and he was suffering from low self-esteem because of it. He was reluctant to give a full smile.

We knew that Christopher had some residual function on the left side of his face. The question now was, how much did he still have? We didn't want to have false hope, but we were gravitating toward a procedure called a cross-facial nerve graft. This technique basically involved a skilled plastic surgeon taking a portion of Christopher's sural nerve from his lower leg and implanting it from the right side of his face to the left. It would act like a little neural highway, originating from the right cheek through the upper lip across to the left cheek. Healing from the procedure would take twelve months. After that period, phase two of the operation would consist of removing a portion of the gracilis muscle from Christopher's inner thigh, transplanting it to the left side of his face, and connecting it to the loose end of the transplanted sural nerve. The procedure's end goal would be to help Christopher achieve improved facial symmetry, since the healthy nerve on the right side of his face would then control the implanted muscle on the left side of his face. The total healing time, from the first surgery to the last, would be thirty months.

In our research, we discovered a prominent surgeon whose work had been featured on national television. Dr. Azizzadeh was the surgeon who had famously restored the facial functioning of a woman who had been shot in the face. We set up a Skype call for the four of us: Christopher, his mother and me, and Dr. Azizzadeh.

We began with a few pleasantries. Then, confident as ever, the doctor asked Christopher to give him a big smile right there as we Skyped. Christopher did so, and Dr. A detected something was off.

"I understand why you are holding back, but there is no need," he said. "Please, try again."

Christopher smiled again, but this time, in an almost ashamed way, he directed his eyes down at the table. Dr. A's response was quick and right to the point. He said, "Christopher, we can help you!"

CHAPTER 10

New School, New Opportunities

———————▼———————

In the spring of Christopher's freshman year, his coach and mentor stepped down from coaching the school's varsity team. Coach Anderson had been an excellent communicator and strategist and his sudden departure left our family even more seriously re-evaluating our commitment to the school. Christopher had been working out with this coach for going on three years, and he loved being on his team. Given this sudden change and the school's inability to handle some very basic accommodations, Jen and I felt the negatives at the school were beginning to outweigh the positives.

To replace Coach Anderson, the following season the school hired a coach who didn't have varsity basketball experience. At the same time, Christopher's hearing in loud gyms had started to regress, and we had arranged to have an interpreter for Christopher in the gym at no cost to the school. These two facts were about to collide.

Michael and Christopher in California

The trouble began one day when I got a phone call at my office at the college informing me that there was a problem. I was told the interpreter "was a distraction and in the way." My first thought was that folks just needed a little education and sensitivity training. Christopher had learned sign language through one of his dual credit courses at the community college, and we believed having the interpreter on the sideline was an obvious accommodation that would help him better understand what the coaching staff was orally communicating. I completely trusted the professionalism of our interpreter. Further, I believed the signing between her and Christopher would become seamless and be totally transparent just like it would be in any school classroom.

I thought about it for a bit, then called the newly hired coach to talk about the situation. First I asked him if it had been communicated that the interpreter was a "distraction and in the way." "Yes," he said. I knew then that the phone call was not going to lead to changes and the conversation ended shortly thereafter.

Following the phone call, I wrote a letter of complaint to the principal. I told Jennifer about it when I got home.

Jennifer was in disbelief. "I don't know how they can even say something like that. They know everything we're doing for Christopher and how much he needs this."

I said, "It might be time to move on. But let's see what kind of response my letter gets."

We told Christopher what had happened. "They just don't get it," he said. It seemed he too was becoming fed up with the school. It had been a deplorable series of events, which was especially upsetting given the religious mission of the school.

When many weeks went by with no intervention toward a resolution, Jen and I made a tough decision. We removed Christopher from the school and the basketball team and transferred him to the local public high school. Christopher had played basketball consistently for the past ten years. It would be very difficult for him to watch the rest of the basketball season go by without playing, but he would be ineligible as a midyear transfer.

Instead of sitting around doing nothing, however, Christopher took his extra time and spent it in the weight room as well as putting things into high gear academically. The end result was that he became quite strong both physically and mentally. In just a few months, Christopher's upper and lower body had already dramatically changed. In fact, his physique had changed so much that even his AAU coach stated later that year that he appeared to be a different person than before. After that year's AAU tryouts, Christopher was selected as one of nine players for a very strong Chicago-area team and continued to recieve state recognition. In the classroom he had already placed himself among the best and the brightest.

With Christopher adjusting to his new high school, Jen and I reflected on his past educational experiences. While we had appreciated some of the spiritual elements of Christopher's previous school, we admitted now that it simply hadn't been the best academic fit for him. We had questioned whether some of his teachers were effectively supporting him, and the constant battle for Christopher's accommodations and the work involved in educating the staff about his needs had, at times, been offensive to me. Add to that the generally distasteful and derogatory remarks that many overzealous fans had made at numerous athletic events. Even the school's athletic director had talked to the vociferous parents! We had observed administrative leadership changes and declining enrollment at our former school as well. All of that turmoil had brought us to this point.

Thankfully, Christopher had comfortably settled into his new school routine and was doing well. As an academic professional, I kicked myself for having previously stereotyped our public high school as a bad fit for Christopher. In reality, his new school had much better accommodations and a faculty and staff group with extensive experience in supporting students with disabilities. Christopher was really enjoying the academic experience at his new school, and he told us directly that he thought the level of instruction in his honors classes was phenomenal.

---------·---------

I sure was glad I had a son who always openly communicated with me. I had listened to other parents talk about their communication experiences with their children, and my relationship with Christopher was worlds apart from what they had described. I knew Christopher's disability was one of the reasons the two of us were so close.

Throughout the years, Christopher's peers had been somewhat disinterested in hanging out with him, and it had led to the two of us doing almost everything together. One can only imagine, then, how excited I was later that year when Christopher began a texting relationship with a girl who lived outside of our town. I was relieved at the thought that a girl from out of town might be a way for Christopher to escape all of the cliques and politics around our home.

After months of continuous texting, Christopher and the girl arranged to have a date at a local restaurant with both her mom and myself in tow. I thought things went great! The lunch atmosphere was somewhat loud, but Christopher's new friend was very cordial to him. Since the lunch had gone so well, Christopher later emailed her and invited her to hang out and play sports with him one Sunday at a local recreation center. Her response was very evasive. First, she told Christopher that she was busy. Then, she said she just wanted to be friends. Finally, she stopped responding to Christopher's emails all together. I did what I could to encourage him. I told him a very nice girl was out there somewhere waiting for him, and she would be beautiful inside and out. "Your future young woman might have her own insecurities and also be unique compared to her friends. But I assure you, you'll meet someone sooner than you think." What I also really believed, however, was that life could just be plain unfair.

I often had tremendous concern when thinking about Christopher's journey and all that he had personally dealt with. Now that his new friend no longer wanted to hang out with him, he began asking me to do even more things with him. I was taking the place of a friend. I passionately wished that the kids who were Christopher's age instead of being closed to interactions with our son, would just allow themselves to be opened. I knew it would make Christopher's life much easier. Christopher was at the halfway point in high school, and I again wondered if college would be better for him.

Christopher had a four-day weekend that fall, so he and I drove ten hours to visit a potential college. The Rochester Institute of Technology (RIT) in New York was a fascinating school located in a metropolitan area that was much larger than that of our home twin cities. Deaf and hearing students came from all over the world to attend school at RIT. It was the first school in the country to have developed a bachelor's degree in software engineering and information technology. We saw, right from the start, that the school had strong academics.

During our visit, Christopher was able to sit in on a software engineering class and also attend one of the school's hockey games. I predicted that Christopher would learn to love hockey if he ended up attending this school! RIT's hockey team had already been to the Frozen Four, which was hockey's equivalent to basketball's Final Four. Christopher seemed to like the school, but not quite as much as I did. On the long ride home I asked him his thoughts. He let me know right out that RIT had a lot of brilliant people going to school there. He also said, "I wonder if I would struggle there academically since I might be coming in after just three years of high school.

"That's possible," I said. "But your new school really understands the critical accommodations you need, both in the classroom and on the basketball floor. That will go a long way." He was quiet and I added, "It all works together, son. Sports is an extension of the learning environment in the classroom with respect to accommodations." Turning to look at him I said, "Your new high school really gets it, and RIT does too."

One of the benefits of RIT was that it would offer Christopher the ability to meet other Deaf students. That aspect, to me, trumped the competing schools. Its basketball program was Division III, but I wondered whether that would even make a difference to Christopher down the road.

⸻▼⸻

That spring, our family took a leap of faith and arranged for Christopher to undergo phase one of his cross-facial nerve graft during spring break. Christopher had already tried out and made the AAU basketball team before his surgery because we knew he would need time to recover. We did not know everything that might come out of the surgery, but we were hopeful the new symmetry in his face would help his self-esteem.

The surgery went well, but when Christopher returned to basketball, he was off balance. The surgeons had taken a branch of a major nerve out of his leg and re-implanted it elsewhere in his body, so this result was not entirely unexpected. Seven weeks after surgery, however, Christopher continued to feel very unbalanced when he ran. Naturally, his playing time went down. Soon he was playing just a few select minutes in his AAU games. Since Christopher was on an elite team that frankly could have competed with many of the high school basketball varsity teams, we all figured he just needed some more time.

It stung Christopher a bit during one big game when his coach sent four players to the scorer's table for substitution and he was left behind to watch from the bench. I glanced over at Christopher, and he looked up at me. I instantly felt his depression transfer to me. He was usually the left-out kid who just wanted to be with the rest of the group, but not on the basketball court. That's where he shined. Unfortunately, he was once again stuck on the outside looking in. An ominous question remained in my mind. What if this is the end of basketball for Christopher? Then the soul searching began. It had been a tremendous run for Christopher, but was it time for him to acknowledge that he had played enough basketball? Was it time for him to move on to other things?

At the end of the basketball season, our focus suddenly shifted. We read in the city newspaper that Christopher's former high school basketball coach had quietly not been rehired for a second year. When the newspaper asked the school why its coach had been let go after just one season, the school administration had no comment. Then, in an extremely bizarre turn of events, the displaced coach attempted to contact me. He said he wanted to explain his thoughts on Christopher. When I intentionally did not return his phone calls or emails, he showed up unannounced at the college where I worked. The front office did not allow him to enter my personal office, but he raised his voice and proceeded forward anyway. As soon as I saw him, I asked him to leave. When he refused to go, I pushed the security button, and Public Safety was at my office within thirty seconds. Needless to say, the staff was pretty shaken up by his behavior, and

Public Safety was concerned enough after interviewing him that they banned him from campus and later fined him as well.

I thought the office incident would be the end of things, but a few days later I received another concerning email from the former coach. It said how great it had been to coach Christopher and that he had just been hired on as a coach at Christopher's new school. It closed by saying that he knew I would want to know that he would once again be coaching Christopher.

I decided to share the email with our college's chief of police. I wanted him to professionally assess the situation and let me know what I was dealing with. Our chief of police had years of both street and college police experience. I had always been impressed with his ability to interact with the students in our community. As an outstanding African American leader, he was considered a role model in the twin cities where we lived. After some discussion, he and I decided that the best solution would be for us to meet with the administration at Christopher's new high school in order to alert them to the situation.

At our meeting, the high school administration assured us that the former coach was in no way involved and definitely not employed as a coach at their school. Simultaneously, the police at my workplace gave me their reports, so I could file a court "no contact" order for everyone in our family. The judge reviewed our request and advised Jen and me to complete some additional documents that would further protect our family. After a lengthy hearing, with the former coach in attendance, the judge ruled he could not have any contact with Christopher, Rachel, me, or Jen for two years. Needless to say, we all felt totally relieved to be away from Christopher's old high school!

Our family received some well-deserved good news at the start of that summer. Christopher's facial nerve was regenerating, and it had started creating nerve impulses in the partially paralyzed portion of the left side of his face. Basketball was also going well for Christopher's team. He finished his AAU season with a trip to the elite eight in Fort Wayne, Indiana. I wish I could say he was back to his old self on the floor but it was still too early for that.

Later that summer, our family talked about Christopher's experience with the new school. In the middle of the discussion, Rachel added her observations. "It seems like the school support services clearly allow you to be the best you can be," she told Christopher. "You seem to be on a more level academic field there." She added, "I think we should stay in the zone with this new high school. They really do get it."

As I reflected on what Rachel said, I knew she too "got it." She had dedicated part of her life to making sure her brother would be treated fairly and could be his best. Jen and I knew too that all that passionate work Rachel put in would pay off for her, and it did. She graduated with honors from the University of Illinois at Urbana-Champaign in just three years with a degree in broadcast journalism. At just twenty years old, she went on to her dream job right out of college with ESPN.

Fully immersed in the new school, Christopher now had an entirely new community of friends, and we had observed that he was feeling more connected. Even though summer had arrived, his social invitations continued to roll in. When we asked Christopher to grade his new school, he quickly stated it was an "A." As the summer wound down, I could see that Christopher was genuinely looking forward to starting his junior year. Or was it his senior year? Although he had just completed his sophomore year, his accumulated credits pushed him toward junior status. His stellar academic record led my wife and me to encourage him to prepare for the ACT. The prep kept him busy over the summer, and I think he liked it that way. By the time the next school year started, he had already achieved one very strong ACT practice score. Our family began considering an early admission application to RIT out east.

As the next school year began, Christopher was excited to attend a girl's birthday party. He said with a grin, "There are only twelve of us going. And I saw on Facebook that twice as many girls as guys were invited."

The evening of the party, Christopher left the house all gussied up, so I knew attending the event was really important for him. Jen, Rachel, and I waited for him to return home and tell us all about the party. Right when Christopher walked in the front door, he asked me to talk with him upstairs. As I followed him up the stairs, I turned around to his sister and mother with a wink to let them know I would report back soon.

When we reached Christopher's room, he showed me a dried rose that he had received from a girl at the party. "So I was just sitting at this party and a girl asks me to step outside. When I went outside, another girl appeared from behind the bushes and gave me this rose, and asked me to go to the homecoming dance with her." He looked a little overwhelmed but elated. Life was good for him again!

Over the next couple of weeks, Christopher was busy gearing up for his homecoming dance. Some friction arose when he found out his date had planned most of the night without seeking his input. Christopher felt kind of like an accessory. He

New high school days

and his date were able to get that straightened out, but his report back from the dance was not very positive: "She spent most of the night talking with her friends instead of me." He said he had spent some of his evening sitting alone. The night left Christopher wondering why his date had even asked him to go to the dance.

I suppose our family should have seen it coming. Early the next week, Christopher's homecoming date asked him to go to lunch. He graciously accepted and even paid for the lunch. On the car ride back to school, however, she told Christopher that they did not have anything in common, and she didn't want to see him again. That car ride was the last time the two of them ever interacted. Christopher viewed her interest in him as a "shallow crush." I found it tough to watch him go through this again, but I admired his positive outlook.

Soon after, Christopher invited a new girl to see a play at the high school. The two of them had a picnic lunch in the car prior to the event. In my mind, Christopher had definitely earned a gold star for creative dating. From all accounts, he and his date had a nice time. Things continued to go so well between the two of them that both of their Facebook pages read "in a relationship" by the end of the month.

It was the calm before a tornado, however, as the young woman suddenly had a change of heart. She stopped paying as much attention to Christopher, and he felt a quiet tension when he was around her. Later, she expressed some mixed messages about her feelings and the drama escalated. At that point Christopher wrote her a letter explaining that he no longer wanted to date her if their relationship continued on in such a confusing manner. Unfortunately, the girl perceived Christopher's heartfelt letter to be a personal attack, and she dumped him. Worse yet, she posted their breakup on Facebook and made it appear to others that Christopher had initiated the end of their relationship.

In an effort to clear the air and also save Christopher's dignity, Jen and I visited the girl's family. As we entered their apartment, the aftermath of the girl's tornado-like activity was apparent. The former girlfriend sat directly in front of us ready to pounce on anything we said. When I attempted to speak, she made it clear that Christopher would learn from this situation and find someone else. Christopher arrived a little later and joined our conversation. The girl's temper once again began to brew when he broached the subject of her confusing communication style. Christopher appeared overwhelmed by her burst of emotion. In the middle of her fury, our family made a quick exit. I couldn't help but look forward to Christopher's future college experiences even more now. I hoped college would put an end to his ongoing streak of opposite-sex rejection.

———▼———

Christopher's fall basketball workouts started up again at school. During basketball games, I noticed that Christopher, in his effort to dive back into things, had started displaying some overtly aggressive behavior on the court. The attitude I observed usually meant he was frustrated. As I watched Christopher's playing, I worried that he would eventually cross the wrong player and a fight would ensue. He had said his back didn't feel fully stable. Was he frustrated about possibly hurting his spine again? To anyone who had seen him on the court in the past, it was clear he wasn't the same player. I wondered where this was leading.

With girl troubles and basketball woes, the high school classroom was a sanctuary for Christopher. Jen and I were almost giddy that Christopher was engaged and interacting well in an oral teaching environment at his new school. Unfortunately, I can't say it was all smooth sailing.

I grew up in the hearing world, so until Christopher came along I had never really given words and language much thought. The Deaf, however, use words and their meanings in an entirely different manner. This was evidenced by an experience Christopher had in his physics class one day. When I heard the story, I knew the whole thing had simply been a misunderstanding of words.

Christopher hadn't done so well on his last physics exam, so he arranged to meet with his teacher after class. He told the teacher which problems he had gotten wrong and the teacher explained the correct answer. After listening to his teacher's explanation, Christopher expressed disbelief regarding his rationale. They started talking about a series of fairly complex mathematical formulas, and things got a little heated when Christopher still wasn't accepting the teacher's explanation. Now, like most hearing people when speaking to Deaf people, the teacher couldn't always tell if Christopher understood what he was saying. For his part, Christopher thought he understood, and to his mind, the rationale just didn't make sense.

When Christopher told me about the argument with his teacher, I pinpointed the problem. It was all just a matter of clearly defining the words being used. The first word was "constant" and the second word was "downstream." I explained to Christopher what the two terms meant in a physics context, and after that he fully understood and accepted the teacher's point of view. He couldn't go back and fix that test result, but at least he would be prepared going forward.

I thought about Christopher's past dating experiences in comparison to his physics issue. I wondered if his dating mishaps had been partially caused by miscommunications between a Deaf person and a hearing person. At that moment, it seemed very clear to me that sign language was another valuable way to enhance future communications between Christopher and the hearing people he communicated with. I was hopeful the sign language courses Christopher had been taking through our community college would lead to even better interpersonal communication in the future.

Dating for sure at any age isn't an easy thing to do. I remembered reading a TV star's article in a national magazine. The star discussed his many futile dating attempts and even mentioned that his wife had at first not paid any attention to him. He finally got his break when she, a friend at the time, left town to do some TV work. It turned out that she had asked him, of all people, to apartment sit for her while she was away. The TV star candidly described himself as having been obese back in the day. Once he was in her apartment, he reorganized her kitchen and stocked it with healthy food. It was a big risk for him, but she was touched by his intervention, and they began dating. He later decided to undergo weight-loss surgery, and the two eventually married. The rest was history.

Similarly, Jen and I had always hoped that people would see around Christopher's disability issues. His lead story was his hearing loss, but his facial paralysis, which affected his self-esteem, was a close second. Now that Christopher had experienced some negative dating situations, his self-confidence appeared to have taken a further hit. With that in mind, Jen and I had been on the lookout for nice and accepting girls for Christopher. We also knew that Christopher would be better off in a more accepting environment, and the Rochester Institute of Technology in New York was just that place.

———

In an effort to keep his school options open and put a shine on his transcript, Christopher decided to substitute senior English for calculus during his junior year. He also submitted his college application to RIT and listed computer science as his potential major. Soon after, the stars aligned and Christopher received a letter from RIT in the mail. He didn't even need to open the envelope since "YOU'RE IN" was written in huge, orange letters on the outside.

Christopher took the weekend to think over his schooling situation. What would he be giving up if he left high school after just three years? What would he gain by attending RIT, a school far away from home but with better resources and a most welcoming environment? Come Monday, he would make the decision to leave high school one year early.

The hardest part of his decision involved telling his varsity teammates and his interpreter that he wouldn't be returning for his senior year. His team had hoped that Christopher would be healthy enough to join them for a state tournament run. And he and his interpreter had stuck together even after their horrendous experience at Christopher's first high school. Now, a great academic school was calling Christopher's name, and it was going to be rich with accommodations for him. RIT had a National Technical Institute for the Deaf, and nearly ten percent of RIT's thirteen thousand students were Deaf. Additionally, Christopher had received both a presidential and a merit scholarship from the institute. From my perspective, it would have been insane for him to have turned the school down.

January 2013 brought Christopher some more exciting news. A new young woman entered his life. The two had actually met in a precalculus class back when Christopher was a sophomore. The cool thing was that they had so many things in common. They were both strong Christians who loved spending time with their families, and they had each earned scholarships to attend terrific universities in their respective fields of study.

Our family was a little hesitant to fully embrace this new girl due to Christopher's past relationship experiences. It seemed almost too good to be true. But their first date said it all. That evening, the two of them spent equal time with each other's families. They ate dinner at one home and enjoyed dessert at the other. When Christopher's new girlfriend arrived at our house, we could really feel a strong Christian spirit within our home. One thing led to another, and by Valentine's Day, Christopher had already posted his new relationship status on Facebook. That coming fall, Christopher would head off to RIT, and his girlfriend would attend a different college some miles away. We all left the relationship up to God's will.

———◆———

It was now spring of 2013, and Christopher's facial symmetry was once again in the spotlight. We had been on this quest since Christopher was just two years old. Many times throughout the years, my wife and I had observed Christopher staring at his one-year-old baby picture, which had been taken before his cochlear implant surgery. We would often hear him say things such as, "That is what my face was supposed to look like." Seeing and hearing that motivated my wife and me to do whatever we could to continue helping Christopher regain a symmetrical face.

This time Christopher, Jen, and I were off again to Beverly Hills for Christopher to undergo yet another eight-hour-long surgery. Dr. Azizzadeh's specific goal for this sur-

*Christopher with Dr. Donald Yoo and
Dr. Babak Azizzadeh*

gery was to take a portion of Christopher's leg muscle, along with its artery, vein, and nerve supply, and connect it to the transplanted nerve and existing vascular supply in the left cheek area of Christopher's face. Our family flew into LAX on a Monday, and Christopher had his pre-op appointment the next day. The pre-op went so well that Christopher's surgery was scheduled for Wednesday. Afterward, he would stay in the same hospital as all the Hollywood stars.

We arrived at the hospital at six o'clock on Wednesday morning, and Jen and I didn't leave until six o'clock that night. Christopher was to remain in the hospital for two more days. When the surgery was completed, there were two drains coming out of Christopher's body. One was behind his ear, and the other was directly out of his inner thigh. Luckily, the NCAA basketball tournament was going on at the same time he was recovering from surgery. All those games from Thursday through the weekend gave us a good diversion from the stressful operation. We all had fun watching the games while Christopher recovered.

After his hospital release, the three of us settled down for the weekend in a townhouse we had rented. During this period, I again found myself reflecting on Christopher's past spinal stress fracture. The injury had never properly healed. Christopher had said his spine felt relatively unstable during that AAU year of play following his injury. I thought it was probably for the best that Christopher had to rest from this surgery because his spine would need to get some additional rest too. Jen and I monitored Christopher's wound drains twelve hours per day, all while watching the NCAA men's basketball tournament. Christopher got in a solid four days of rest at the townhouse before he headed to his post-op appointment. There, the doctor removed the drain tube from his leg but left the one in his face until we returned home to the Midwest.

Christopher went back to school once the last drain was removed, and my wife and I wondered how his final term would go. A number of Christopher's peers were planning on trying out for the school's Mr. Charger Contest. It was a nutty contest that all of the buff male wanna-bes entered. It consisted of beauty, talent, and question and answer categories. The goal of the contest was to find out which young man had the right stuff. On a practical level, Christopher hoped that all his facial swelling from the surgery would go down before the night of the big contest.

Once Christopher found out what the prize for winning the Mr. Charger Contest was, he was all in. The winner would receive two prom tickets and a free tuxedo rental. In classic Christopher form, he asked the principal if he could donate the prize back to a needy student if he won. The competition was fierce that night. Unbeknownst to the audience, Christopher creatively used his FM system from the classroom to correctly guess a random person's artwork that had been drawn behind his back without him looking. Then, he carefully articulated the importance of diversity at the school during the question and answer session. He managed to do all of this while looking spectacular in his rented tuxedo!

In the end, a student rapper brought home the prize. It was a small disappointment, but given that student's financial situation, our family was so grateful he would receive help with the prom. As we left the building to go home, the theater department director approached Christopher. She said she thought his magic trick was very cool, and she also loved his answer during the question and answer category. She gave him a warm smile. "You should have won," she said. Christopher smiled back and said, "Nah, I actually think the best person won."

In the car, Christopher explained that if he had won the contest, he would have chosen to donate his winnings to the exact same type of student who had won. Christopher had—and has—such a good heart. He wished that more needy students could get that kind of assistance.

The school year was starting to wind down and Christopher had just entered the seven-week post-surgery stage when the other shoe dropped. It started on a Tuesday with what appeared to be a small pimple on Christopher's left cheek. By Friday that pimple had escalated into a bump the size of a golf ball. Not even a strong antibiotic could help that bump. After Jen and I consulted with Dr. Azizzadeh in California, we were advised to take Christopher to see the local ENT specialist on call. The ENT determined it was most likely an infection. She considered it to be serious enough that she scheduled Christopher for another surgery the very next morning. All the while, our family worried about whether Christopher's newly implanted muscle could withstand this new development.

I slept in Christopher's room that night in a side chair so he wouldn't have to be alone. For obvious reasons, I didn't get much rest at all. Christopher's surgery began in the late morning. At noon, Jen and I were told things went very well. The golf ball–sized bump on Christopher's face had in fact been infectious material. The surgeon had drained the puss, which resolved the infection but left Christopher with a large bandage covering his face. It was now also the Saturday of prom, and Christopher was unable to attend due to further risk of infection.

Christopher's prom date took the bad news wonderfully. We told Christopher to dress up. His date then arrived at the hospital in her prom dress to take pictures with him. My wife and I made the best of things and headed out to dinner so the prom couple could have some alone time. The following day Christopher was released from the hospital, and his school graciously adjusted his final exam schedule to fit his medical situation.

Christopher's high school days came to a close with a series of graduation parties. His large number of party invites revealed that he had also successfully connected with the senior class even though he technically should only have been a junior. Our family held a blockbuster of a graduation party at our house just prior to Christopher's ceremony at the U of I's basketball arena. Over seventy students, doctors, teachers, therapists, relatives, coaches, neighbors, and colleagues came by our house to wish Christopher well. The party culminated in a twenty-five-minute montage video that spanned the course of Christopher's life. When it was over, there wasn't a dry eye in the place. The staff from the Swann Center where Christopher had volunteered for the past ten years left the best graduation card. It was very special to Christopher because all of the center's residents whose lives had been touched by him had signed the card. While each of the residents had left only a sort of scribble, our family was moved to see all of those unique markings offered just for Christopher. We had to call Christopher's ten years of Saturday volunteering what it was: legendary.

———▼———

With graduation behind them, Christopher and his girlfriend were at the point where they would be moving in opposite directions to attend college. While the two of them were clearly in love, the reality was that their schools were ten hours apart. I got the feeling they both wanted to try to make the long-distance relationship work. At the same time, hearing Christopher's girlfriend tell him that everything would be "okay" made me think that their transition would be a tough one. I hoped everything would go well for them. I didn't want either one to emotionally hurt.

Not long after graduation, Christopher, in his own way, expressed to me that his girlfriend seemed less communicative to him. When he tried to discuss the issue with her, she was overly flip to him. In his mind, her behavior was less than acceptable communication, and she had one strike against her.

Unfortunately, strike number two followed very quickly. This time I was there to witness the encounter. While in the car with me, Christopher and his girlfriend were discussing issues related to harassment and stalking. Christopher decided to tell her the story about his past protective order against a former coach. Although our family had only shared this horrendous experience with very close friends and professional colleagues, I was happy that Christopher felt comfortable enough to share it with his girlfriend. After hearing the story, however, she said his former coach had probably just been focused on running his practice. Christopher and I were shocked by her insensitive response. How could she not understand that Christopher's accommodations at basketball practices were an extension of the classroom learning environment?

Her response troubled me. Jen and I had always believed that support was a critical piece in all of Christopher's relationships. I decided to take a risk. A few days later, I asked his girlfriend if she would be willing to ask Christopher to tell her the entire story about his former basketball experience. "You owe Christopher an apology for being flippant before," I added. To my great relief, she agreed. Christopher accepted her apology and told her the full story, and the two of them remained inseparable for the remainder of the summer.

A lot of closure was rapidly taking place in Christopher's life. He had been a Division I college basketball recruit at one point in his career. He had gone to the state tournament final four and the elite eight, and he had advanced to sectional play in all his other years of playing hoops. Christopher's guidance counselor just prior to graduation described him as "one of the finest students to have ever attended this high school."

Now Christopher had both a presidential scholarship and a merit award to RIT tucked under his belt, and he was looking forward to a fantastic college opportunity. He just had to get through a five-hour, summer college calculus course before he would be ready for all the computer science challenges at RIT in the fall.

———▾———

August quickly snuck up on Christopher. He had spent most of his summer working part-time at our community college and studying. In mid-August, he and his girlfriend said their good-byes on the RIT campus. Christopher, the gentleman he was, gave gifts to all his girlfriend's family members before he bid them each a fond farewell. I could see from the look on his face that he was unsure of when he would see them again.

When one door closed, another one widely opened. Christopher met his new roommate during RIT's freshman orientation. His roommate was also Deaf and had grown up in a mainstreamed school in the Midwest just like Christopher. Minnesota, ya know! The orientation was amazing. Christopher got to meet all of the other academic scholarship students at a luncheon, and I could see that things were going to be great for him.

RIT's orientation lasted a solid seven days, and the school was simply magnificent! The college had complete audiology support for students with cochlear implants. As an academic professional, I knew these accommodation services were exemplary. Our family felt even more engaged the more we experienced RIT. We all knew the school would be an excellent place for Christopher to call his new home.

The world was now Christopher's oyster. My wife and I said a tearful good-bye to him in a triangular hug. As I watched Christopher and his roommate walk away to go to the next orientation session, I suddenly felt a sense of peace. The dream of the path of our esoteric journey to "be opened" came true. I looked back over my shoulder and glimpsed Christopher's implant catching a ray of sun on the left side of his head. His roommate's implant was perfectly aligned on the right side of his head. So there the two of them were, like bookends, as they walked and easily conversed with one another. At that very moment, Christopher stopped and turned to see us watching him. He signed, "I love you," and pointed to us. Jen and I signed the same back to him, and with that final sign to our son, the words of Mark 7:34 resonated in my head.

> *They brought to him a deaf man who had an impediment in his speech;*
> *and they begged him to lay his hand on him.*
> *He took him aside in private, away from the crowd,*
> *and put his fingers into his ears, and he spat and touched his tongue.*
> *Then looking up to heaven, he sighed and said to him,*
> *"Ephphatha," that is, "Be opened." And immediately his ears were opened,*
> *his tongue was released, and he spoke plainly.*

EPILOGUE

▼

C hristopher entered the B. Thomas Golisano College of Computing and Informational Sciences at Rochester Institute of Technology in New York in the fall of 2013. While at RIT he studied web and mobile computing with a concentration in human computer interaction and ubiquitous computing, along with an immersion in Deaf cultural studies.

Throughout his college career, Christopher continued to be extensively involved in his community. He was active in both the Newman and Cru campus ministries and was also a member of Sigma Chi fraternity. He served RIT's residential life program as a resident advisor for three straight years on campus.

Christopher meeting with the "Father of the Internet," Dr. Vint Cerf

During his junior and senior years, he was a research assistant and later a teaching assistant for the College of Computing. He also secured highly sought after summer internships in New York, Washington, D.C., and Lincoln, Nebraska. His summer project work encompassed user-centered research and design in areas of commercial business, government, and sports world technologies.

Christopher is extremely proud of his research work in the Linguistic and Assistive Technologies Laboratory at RIT. He believes that innovation in linguistic technologies and computer interaction could empower and create more possibilities for people. He hopes that, through his efforts, the lives of people with disabilities will also be made easier through accessibility applications. Christopher graduated cum laude from RIT in May of 2017.

Christopher accepted a fellowship and began his first year of graduate school at Cornell University in August of 2017.

The odds were 1 in 3,500 that Christopher would be born the way he was: Deaf. In his mind, he had always believed life would continue to get better for him because he learned to play the cards he was given with the faith that his esoteric journey would eventually be opened. Indeed, he knew the truth.

THOMAS HOPKINS GALLAUDET STATUE

In Christopher's hometown there is a statue that epitomizes his journey. The plaque beneath the statue states:

Thomas Hopkins Gallaudet is best remembered as the founding father of American Deaf education. Gallaudet, inspired by the sharp mind of young Deaf Alice Cogswell, traveled to Europe in 1815 in search of a teaching method for the Deaf. There he recruited a highly educated Deaf person, Laurent Clerc, a teacher at the Paris School for the Deaf. On the voyage back to America, Clerc taught Gallaudet the language of signs. In return, Gallaudet taught Clerc the English language. This unique relationship between a hearing and a Deaf man marks the beginning of Deaf education in the United States. With Clerc as a model, Gallaudet succeeded in convincing the American public that Deaf children were educable and could become teachers themselves. Gallaudet founded the first permanent school for the Deaf in Hartford, Connecticut, in 1817. Later, Gallaudet married a Deaf woman, Sophia Fowler. Their son, Edward Minor, went on to establish a college for the Deaf, later named Gallaudet University in honor of his father, Thomas Hopkins.

Plaque at the University of Illinois at Urbana-Champaign

Thomas Hopkins Gallaudet and Alice Cogswell

Made in the USA
Monee, IL
06 January 2020